Alien Adventures

Teaching Handbook Year 3–4/P4–5

Lindsay Pickton & Christine Chen

OXFORD
UNIVERSITY PRESS

Project X *Alien Adventures* Team

Series Consultants: Catherine Baker, Jennifer Chew, Maureen Lewis, Janice Pimm, Linda Tallent

Scottish Curriculum consultant: Gill Friel
Welsh Curriculum consultant: Pat Griffiths
Northern Ireland Curriculum consultant: Rachel Russ
Inside cover notes and PCMs: Christine Cork
Illustrations by: Jonatronix Ltd.

Project X concept by Rod Theodorou and Emma Lynch

The publisher wishes to thank the following schools for their valuable contribution to the trialling and development of **Project X *Alien Adventures*:** Birtley East Community Primary School, County Durham; Eastry Church of England Primary School, Sandwich; Featherby Infant and Nursery School, Gillingham; Goldington Green Lower School, Bedford; Halebank CE (VC) Primary School, Widnes; Kirkby Church of England Primary School, Kirkby; Lakeside Primary School, Camberley; Larkrise Primary School, Oxford; Littleton Green Primary School, Cannock; Newsham Primary School, Blyth; Walton Oak Primary School, Walton-on-Thames; Wickhambreaux CE Primary School, Canterbury.

Max   Cat   Nok   Ant   Tiger

OXFORD
UNIVERSITY PRESS

Great Clarendon Street, Oxford, OX2 6DP,
United Kingdom

Oxford University Press is a department of the University of Oxford.
It furthers the University's objective of excellence in research, scholarship,
and education by publishing worldwide. Oxford is a registered trade mark of
Oxford University Press in the UK and in certain other countries

© Oxford University Press 2014
First Edition published in 2014

All rights reserved. No part of this publication may be reproduced, stored in a retrieval system, or transmitted, in any form or by any means, without the prior permission in writing of Oxford University Press, or as expressly permitted by law, by licence or under terms agreed with the appropriate reprographics rights organization. Enquiries concerning reproduction outside the scope of the above should be sent to the Rights Department, Oxford University Press, at the address above.

You must not circulate this work in any other form
and you must impose this same condition on any acquirer
British Library Cataloguing in Publication Data
Data available

978-0-19-839145-6

1 3 5 7 9 10 8 6 4 2

Paper used in the production of this book is a natural, recyclable product made from wood grown in sustainable forests. The manufacturing process conforms to the environmental regulations of the country of origin.

Printed in Great Britain by Bell and Bain

Acknowledgements

Character illustrations by Jonatronix Ltd

Photocopy master illustrations by Nathalie Ortega

Project X concept by Rod Theodorou and Emma Lynch

The publisher would like to thank the following for permission to reproduce photographs:
p14 Monkey Business Images/Shutterstock; **p17** Hasloo Group Production Studio /Shutterstock; **p18** Monkey Business Images/Shutterstock; **p20** Monkey Business Images/Shutterstock; **p24** Monkey Business Images/Shutterstock; **p32** Olesya Feketa/Shutterstock; **p35** OUP/photodisk; **p37** Michael Garton; **p43** Jorge Santillan, All other images © Oxford University Press.

MIX
Paper from responsible sources
FSC
www.fsc.org FSC® C007785

Contents

Welcome to Project X	4
Blast off with Project X *Alien Adventures*!	6
Project X *Alien Adventures* structure chart	8
Getting the most out of Project X *Alien Adventures*	10
Giving boys a reason to read	14
The importance of independent reading at Year 3–4/P4–5	17
Creating a whole-school culture of independent reading	19
Independent reading in the classroom	21
The importance of talk, reading aloud and reading partners	24
Reading partner prompt sheet	29
Independent reading and comprehension at Year 3–4/P4–5	30
The interdependence of reading and writing	33
Partnership with parents and carers	35
Bedroom door hanger	38
About Project X *Alien Adventures* in Year 3–4/P4–5	39
Observation, assessment and planning: Year 3–4/P4–5	44
• The Oxford Ros Wilson Criterion Scale for Reading	45
• Reading assessment record: Lower Key Stage 2	53
• Project X *Alien Adventures*: vocabulary, punctuation and grammar: Year 3–4/P4–5	54
Reading and writing certificates	58
Project X *Alien Adventures* and the Scottish Curriculum for Excellence	60
Project X *Alien Adventures* and the National Literacy Framework in Wales	66
Project X *Alien Adventures* and the Northern Ireland Curriculum	69
Photocopiable Masters	73

Welcome to Project X

Project X is the overarching name for a series of highly engaging and effective reading programmes published by Oxford University Press. As well as the brand new **Project X Alien Adventures** programme for independent reading, the series includes a comprehensive, whole-school guided reading programme (the original 'Project X' – Project X ORIGINS), a small, focused phonics programme (Project X PHONICS), and a reading intervention programme (Project X CODE). Drawing on research evidence, classroom practice and a real understanding of what makes modern children tick, it has everything you need to make learning both effective and fun.

The materials that make up **Project X** have been developed with the very best educational experts.

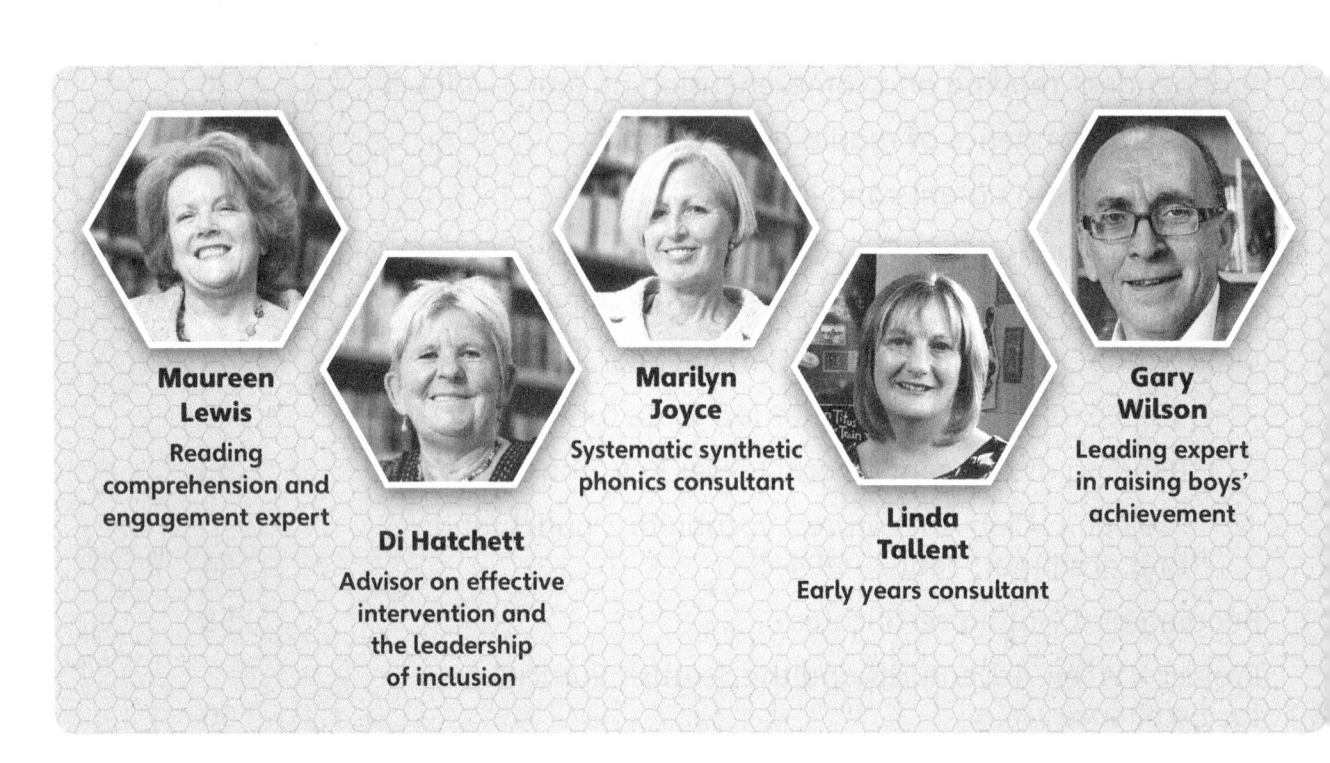

Maureen Lewis — Reading comprehension and engagement expert

Di Hatchett — Advisor on effective intervention and the leadership of inclusion

Marilyn Joyce — Systematic synthetic phonics consultant

Linda Tallent — Early years consultant

Gary Wilson — Leading expert in raising boys' achievement

What makes Project X unique?

All of the programmes within Project X share the same aim: to motivate and raise the achievement of 21st century children, especially boys.

This doesn't mean that **Project X** isn't for girls – far from it. What it does mean is that, unlike any other reading programme, **Project X** provides teaching and learning resources explicitly designed to support boys, whilst not disadvantaging girls.

The gender gap in achievement in reading and writing is something many schools still need to address, with white, working-class boys at the greatest disadvantage.

According to the Ofsted framework, schools will be judged on how they respond to the needs of particular groups of pupils by observing how well they make progress and fulfill their potential. Boys' achievement comes under this guideline. It is imperative, therefore, to try and help to close the gender gap.

Welcome to Project X

Project X Phonics
Engaging group reading with a phonics focus
Reception/P1–Year 1/P2
40 fiction and non-fiction books

Origins
Effective guided reading starts here!
Reception/P1–Year 6/P7
Over 200 books

Alien Adventures
Blast off on an incredible independent reading journey!
Reception/P1–Year 4/P5
96 books

CODE
A breakthrough for SEN and struggling readers
Provides rapid catch-up for children from Year 2 onwards. 56 books

There is a wealth of research evidence to show that boys, far more than girls, require specific strategies to engage them with learning. 'Boy-friendly books' are a big part of the appeal of **Project X**, but they are only part of the solution to engaging boys. The series also draws on a wealth of evidence from research, case studies and various Raising Boys' Achievement initiatives to provide teachers with strategies and approaches that are proven to be effective with boys. What's more, having engaged boys in the classroom gives teachers more time to ensure that every child is being helped to progress at the right pace. And some girls can really benefit from the lively, imaginative conversations that engaged boys participate in.

The other unique feature of **Project X** is the original, exciting character adventure that sits at the heart of the series from Reception/P1 right through to Year 6/P7. Readers can follow the varied adventures of Max, Cat, Ant and Tiger – four ordinary children with extraordinary watches that allow them to shrink to micro-size. Research shows that familiar characters are the number one hook for young readers, particularly boys, and because the characters evolve and have different adventures **Project X** offers both familiarity and variety. As well as engaging children with reading, these characters and stories provide children with a wealth of stimulus for talk and writing … and even playground play! The characters also give children common ground – whatever their age, ability or level of achievement, every child could be reading a **Project X** book, talking about the characters and sharing their experiences with their friends.

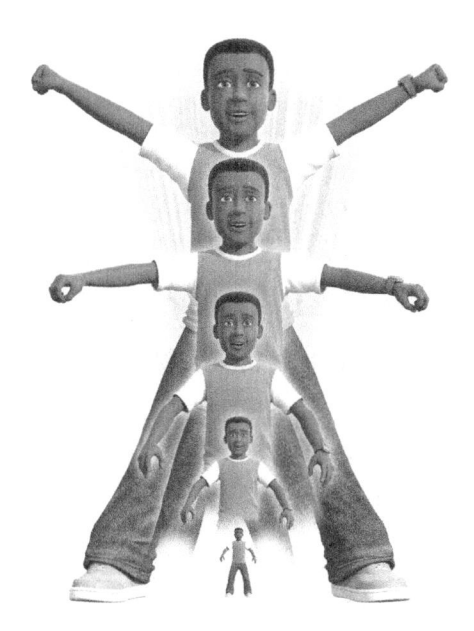

Find out more about *Big Writing Adventures*

Oxford University Press has been working with Ros Wilson to develop an exciting new writing programme for Years 2–6/Primary 3–7. *Big Writing Adventures* combines the powerful **Big Writing** methodology with a series of highly engaging 'writing missions', some of which involve the **Project X** characters. For schools in England, the programme also provides valuable clarity of progression through the new English curriculum.

Visit www.oxfordprimary.co.uk to find out more.

Blast off with Project X *Alien Adventures!*

Join Max, Cat, Ant and Tiger as they embark on an exciting new independent reading journey!

Project X *Alien Adventures* offers 96 amazing new stories, featuring Max, Cat, Ant and Tiger … and some new alien friends! Highly motivating, fully decodable, and with finer steps of progression than any other reading programme, these books are a great way to build children's confidence and enthusiasm and are ideal for independent reading.

The **Project X *Alien Adventures*** series fully supports the new National Curriculum. The curriculum stresses the importance of pupils having access to reading books that are consistent with their developing phonic knowledge and skills; it also states that: 'At the same time they will need to hear, share and discuss a wide range of high-quality books to develop a love of reading and broaden their vocabulary'.

Books they CAN read independently

The **Project X *Alien Adventures*** books are 100% decodable: the series follows a progressive systematic synthetic phonics structure, which correlates to *Letters and Sounds* Phases 1 to 6. In Reception/P1 and Year 1/P2, children have the chance to consolidate and practise the concepts and skills they have learned in their daily phonics sessions. The small steps of progression and fine levelling ensure that all children experience reading success right from the very beginning. In later books, Years 2–4 (P3–5), the careful levelling continues, building children's stamina, fluency and comprehension skills and ensuring that they develop as confident and 'hungry' readers.

Books they WANT to read and will love reading

Project X *Alien Adventures* is 100% fun. The series combines all the best ingredients of **Project X**: the stunning 3D artwork, the continuous plot and engaging stories, and the well-loved characters with some great new aliens, gadgets and vehicles.

FREE online resources! Visit www.oxfordprimary.co.uk for lots of **Project X *Alien Adventures*** freebies, including: animations, bookmarks, door hangers and the new *Alien Adventures* game!

The *Alien Adventures* story

Our adventures start when Nok, a micro-sized alien from Planet Exis, crash-lands on Earth. He soon meets four micro-sized children – Max, Cat, Ant and Tiger – who teach him about life on Earth. In later books our heroes find Nok's spaceship and blast off into space! So begins their series of action-packed, intergalactic adventures. Together, the micro-friends travel to Planet Exis, where they come up against a space villain called Badlaw and his army of robotic Krools. Our heroes then find out that they have to go on a mission to collect four fragments that form the Core of Exis in order to defeat Badlaw and save the galaxy! For more about the **Project X *Alien Adventures*** story in Year 3–4/P4–5, see pages 39–43.

Project X *Alien Adventures* structure chart

Year	Oxford Level	Book Band		Letters and Sounds Phase	*Alien Adventures* books	*Alien Adventures* series companions	Teachers' Resources
Reception/Primary 1	1	Pre-Book Bands Lilac	A	Phase 1	• Max's Box • In the Sky		Teaching Handbook Reception/P1
			B	Phase 2, Set 1	• Splat! • Max's Rocket		
	1+	1 Pink	A	Phase 2, Set 2	• The Fishing Trip • Let's Bake!		
			B	Phase 2, Set 3	• Tin Cat • Sit, Cog Dog!		
			C	Phase 2, Set 4	• Get Ant! • Peg It Up		
			D	Phase 2, Set 5	• Run, Tin Cat! • Peck, Peck		
	2	2 Red	A	Phase 3, Set 6	• An Odd Bug • Nok Can Fix It		
			B	Phase 3, Set 7	• Cat's Picnic • A Bag of Tricks		
			C	Phase 3	• Moths! • Tiger's Fish		
	3	3 Yellow	A	Phase 3	• On Nok's Trail • I Win!		
			B	Phase 3	• Popcorn Surfing • Stuck in the Mud		
			C	Phase 3	• The Lost Cow • The Rocket Flight		
Year 1/Primary 2	4	4 Light Blue	A	Phase 4	• Cat's Painting • It's Too Hot!		Teaching Handbook Year 1/P2
			B	Phase 4	• Helter-Skelter • Funfair Fun		
			C	Phase 4	• A Shock for Nok • Goal!		
	5	5 Green	A	Phase 5	• The Seagull • Claws		
			B	Phase 5	• The Parachute • Molly's New Toy		
			C	Phase 5	• Nok's Lunch • Nok Gets Homesick		
	6	6 Orange	A	Phase 5	• An Amazing Find • Blast Off!		
			B	Phase 5	• Don't Press the Buttons! • Worm Song		
			C	Phase 5	• Spacewalk • The Junk Cruncher		

Primary/P references in this handbook relate to Primary year groups in Scotland and Northern Ireland.

Year	Oxford Level	Book Band	Letters and Sounds Phase	Alien Adventures books	Alien Adventures series companions	Teachers' Resources
Year 2/Primary 3	7	7 Turquoise	Phase 6	• Planet Exis • Attack of the Buzzles • The Empty Palace • Battle with the Beast • Nurp Stampede • The Trap	Alien Adventures Companion 2	Teaching Handbook Year 2/P3
	8	8 Purple	Phase 6	• Tiger x 4 • The Sands of Akwa • Holo-board Havoc • Ant's Pact • The Screams of the Raptiss • The Secret Whirlpool		
	9	9 Gold	Phase 6	• The Crystal Planet • The Ruby Cage • The Hunt for Nok • Race to the Pyramid • One Step Ahead • Chamber of Treasures		
	10	10 White	Phase 6	• Swamp Crash • Spaceship Graveyard • Fear Forest • Attack of the Giant Meeb • The Cave of Life • Save the World!		
	11	11 Lime		• Space Hunt • The Deadly Cave • Grumptus Attack • The Mines of Moxor • The Contest • Return to Exis		
Year 3/Primary 4	9	12 Brown		• The Destroyer • Space Rat Rescue • Crunch Time! • The Moon Winder	Alien Adventures Companion 3	Teaching Handbook Years 3–4/P4–5
	10			• Space Vultures • The Planet of Bones • Starmite Swarm • The Giants of Ariddas		
	11			• The Craggrox Awake • Attack of the Blobs • The Image Maker • Battle with Badlaw		
Year 4/Primary 5	12	13 Grey		• Badlaw's Revenge • The Rats of Rolia • Trapped in Time • Double Cross		
	13			• The Rust Monster • Pit-stop Peril • The Red Cutlass • Cyberbee Break Out		
	14			• Operation Holotanium • An Ancient Enemy • The Fury of Vogoss • The Waythroo Wormhole		

Project X Alien Adventures structure chart

Getting the most out of Project X *Alien Adventures*

The **Project X** *Alien Adventures* books are designed and levelled to support children's independent reading – either within school or at home – allowing them to practise and consolidate vital skills, build stamina and fluency, and develop that all-important love of reading right from day one. The series couldn't be easier to use.

Step 1: Get your children on board!

Animations are a great way to engage 21st-century children, especially boys! Launch **Project X** *Alien Adventures* in your classroom with one of our short animations. These are a great stimulus for talk as they give a flavour of the adventures to come, much like a movie trailer, and can really help to generate a 'buzz' around the series. There are two animations, both of which are available free, online at **www.oxfordprimary.co.uk**.

Animation 1

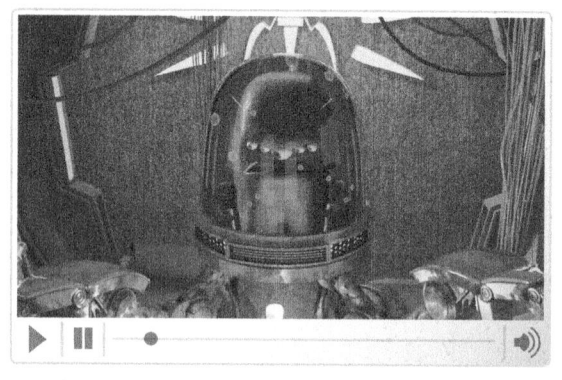

Animation 2

Step 2: Check out the *Alien Adventures* Companions

Accompanying the **Project X** *Alien Adventures* series are 3 companions designed to really hook children in and make them want to read the stories themselves. They give readers additional information about the special watches, the characters, the spaceship, spacesuits and gadgets, as well as comic strip adventures, jokes, games and things to make and do. They are perfect for generating talk … and perfect for wet breaktimes!

Step 3: Choose a reading book

The **Project X** *Alien Adventures* series is correlated to Book Bands, *Letters and Sounds* Phases (where appropriate) and the Oxford Levels so you and your pupils can organize, store and select books quickly and easily. The assessment record sheets in this handbook will help you identify the Book Band/Oxford Level a child is comfortable reading at so that you can direct their book choice accordingly.

> ### Should I choose books for pupils or allow free choice?
>
> You know your children best and will often want to choose books that are at a level that is right for them. However, it is also important to give children a sense that they can freely choose their own books. These might be from the relevant Book Band/Oxford Level or from a wider library selection.
>
> If they sometimes want to just pick up a book and look at the pictures, or read a favourite 'easy' book, that's OK. The important thing is they are still getting a positive experience. Children need to choose any book they want in the classroom and *have a go* at it. They need to read fully-decodable books, familiar favourites and more challenging texts to develop fluency and a love of reading.

Step 4: Talk about the book

The importance of spoken language for developing pupils' vocabulary, grammar and understanding for reading and writing is given high priority in the National Curriculum. On the inside front and back cover of every **Project X** *Alien Adventures* book, you will find notes which: give question prompts and points for discussion, point out the challenge words, and give additional activities that children can do. Children might do these activities with their peers, with an adult in school or with a parent/carer at home.

Step 5: Do a follow-up activity

For each book in the series there is a corresponding Photocopiable Master (PCM), which can be used for follow-up work to develop formative comprehension skills. There are also more generic PCMs for additional practice.

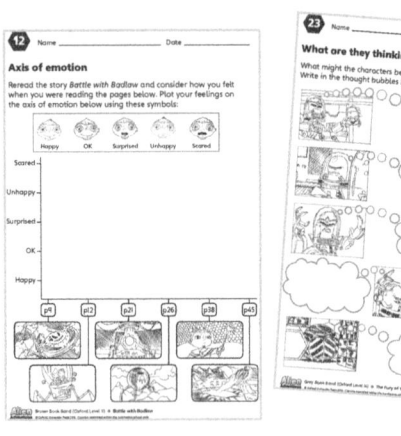

Step 6: Assessment

Support for assessing pupil progress against the requirements of the Early Years Foundation Stage, *Letters and Sounds* for phonics and the National Curriculum (as appropriate) is provided in the Teaching Handbooks. See pages 44–57 for more information.

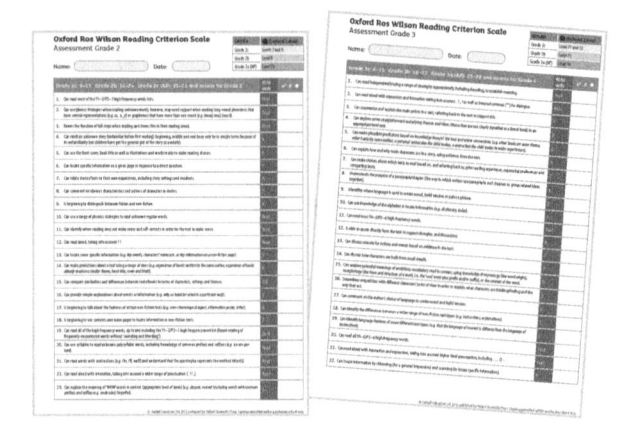

Free online resources

Visit: **www.oxfordprimary.co.uk** for other free *Alien Adventures* resources:
- bookmarks
- door hangers
- PCMs
- the **Project X** *Alien Adventures* game!

Professional development

For advice and top tips on developing early independent readers and working with parents as partners, watch the films by early years expert Linda Tallent free, online at: **www.oxfordprimary.co.uk**.

Supporting parents and carers

On the inside front and back cover of every book, you will find notes which: give question prompts and points for discussion, highlight phonic practice words, point out the challenge words, and give follow-up activities that parents and children can do together.

eBooks and online support

Oxford University Press' award-winning website is packed with expert advice, top tips and activities to help families support their children with reading and maths at home. It has a collection of **free eBooks**, including **Project X *Alien Adventures*** titles. Visit **www.oxfordowl.co.uk** to find out more.

For more advice on working with parents, see pages 16 and 35–38 of this handbook.

Giving boys a reason to read

Project X *Alien Adventures* has been created to meet the needs and interests of all children. However, there is a wealth of research showing that there are specific challenges involved in ensuring some boys become readers. Boys are more likely than girls to struggle with reading and to give up on independent reading. For these reasons **Project X** *Alien Adventures* has been designed to include content that will particularly motivate boys to read, while also appealing to girls.

Why do some boys struggle with reading?

The reasons for some boys' underperformance in literacy are complex and often include wider societal factors such as gender roles and stereotypes, family influences, behaviour issues, peer pressure and self-stereotyping. There are also factors relating directly to the teaching of reading such as boys' early reading experiences, teacher expectations, teaching and learning practices, learning contexts and book choice. One factor, however, stands out above all others when it comes to boys and learning, and that is *motivation*. When it comes to reading and writing boys, far more than girls, need to see a clear purpose for what they are doing. They won't simply do something because they are told to; they want to know what's in it for them. For some boys it's not that they can't, it's just that they can't be bothered!

Building identity

Readers can confirm and extend their own identity through reading and so build their confidence. The **Project X** characters think, act and feel in ways that modern children, particularly boys, will be able to relate to. However, they do not represent gender stereotypes. They show both active and affective aspects of identity. *Alien Adventures* also has a strong emphasis on teamwork. So, even though the stories themselves may be fantastical, readers can empathize with the characters and make links to their own lives.

Encouraging talk

Talking about and reflecting on books is a vital part of becoming a reader and talking to gather ideas is an important strategy for becoming a mark-maker/writer. Boys in particular benefit from articulating and reinforcing their thoughts and ideas through talk.

The National Curriculum stresses the importance of spoken language across the whole curriculum. The **Project X** *Alien Adventures* series can be used as a stimulus to support talk in a number of ways:

1. by watching the free online animations,
2. through use of the companion books,
3. through discussion around the exciting stories and on-going narrative,
4. through the in-book features, such as the *Fact file* pages from Year 1/P2 onwards,
5. by using the inside cover notes,
6. through follow-up activities.

ICT and multimedia

Today's children are growing up in a multimedia world. Research has shown that multimedia is an excellent way of engaging boys with literacy. As well as being highly engaging and motivating for children, films, cartoons, websites, computer games and other multimedia texts often present specific and sophisticated literacy challenges. It is important that pupils' experience in using such forms of literacy is acknowledged, appreciated and developed if they are to be fully literate in the 21st century.

Project X *Alien Adventures* responds to this in four ways.

1. The series aims to engage young readers by using a detailed, 3D digital illustration style in all the stories. This brings the world of films and computer games to books and has been a huge hit with children.
2. **Project X** *Alien Adventures* offers a number of eBooks that can be accessed online and used to engage children, stimulate discussion, and support both traditional and multimedia literacy skills.
3. The *Alien Adventures* animations can be used to introduce the series in a class session, which can help build anticipation and generate a 'buzz' around reading independently.
4. The *Alien Adventures* Companions encourage wider reading by providing additional information about the characters, gadgets and vehicles in a format that children will be familiar with from 'annuals' that accompany popular television series.

To access the FREE eBooks or watch the **Project X** *Alien Adventures* animations visit:
www.oxfordprimary.co.uk

Purposeful learning and regular reviews of progress

Boys like to have a clear purpose in order to understand their reason for learning. They also like to see evidence of their progress, as they find achievement and recognition motivating. **Project X** *Alien Adventures* takes the reader through small steps of progression and fine levelling as a way of ensuring boys experience success as readers from the very beginning.

Family involvement and reading role models

Parents/carers are important partners in helping children become readers and writers. It is important, for example, for boys to see others – particularly other males – reading. This reinforces the place that reading has in society and therefore the reasons for learning to read.

Teachers have a key role to play in working in partnership with parents to support their young children. Supporting families in building a reading culture at home is important so that boys see reading as something to engage with beyond the school setting/environment. Involving fathers or other males in reading with boys has been shown to be one successful way to encourage this. On the inside covers of each of the **Project X** *Alien Adventures* books there are some simple questions and activities to support parents/carers in reading with their children. For more information on working with parents, see pages 35–38.

> **Oxford OWL**
>
> **For teachers**
> Helping you with free eBooks, inspirational resources, advice and support
>
> **For parents**
> Helping your child's learning with free eBooks, essential tips and fun activities
>
> **www.oxfordowl.co.uk**

Competitive approaches and celebrating achievement

Much of the research into raising boys' achievement shows that competitive approaches to learning can be effective. This doesn't mean setting children against each other but against their own personal targets. In each of the **Project X** *Alien Adventures* Teaching Handbooks (Rec–Year 2/P1–3), you will find a number of 'I can' statements to support pupils with monitoring their own success.

On-going praise, together with recognition and reward for success are vitally important to young learners, particularly boys. There are reading and writing certificate templates in each handbook that can be used to celebrate achievement.

> **FREE: Getting the Best out of Boys Kit**
>
> We've teamed up with Gary Wilson, one of the UK's leading experts on raising boys' achievement, to create a professional development kit for schools to help you get the best out of your boys. Visit **www.oxfordprimary.co.uk** to find out more.

The importance of independent reading at Year 3–4/P4–5

There is increasing national and international research pointing to the reciprocal relationship between reading frequency, reading enjoyment and attainment.

- *Evidence suggests that there is a positive relationship between reading frequency, reading enjoyment and attainment.* (Clark 2011; Clark and Douglas, 2011).[1]
- *Regularly reading stories or novels outside of school is associated with higher scores in reading assessments.* (PIRLS, 2006; PISA, 2009).[2]
- *There is a positive link between positive attitudes towards reading and scoring well on reading assessments.* (Twist et al, 2007).[3]

The entrance into Key Stage 2 is a pivotal point in a child's perception of him/herself as a reader: it is feasible that two children might leave KS1 with similar reading levels yet with widely differing experiences and attitudes to reading; while one child may have experienced guided success, enthusiastically and systematically moving through reading schemes, seldom choosing to read unprompted, another child assessed at the same level may have developed a real passion for reading, choosing to read for pleasure beyond what's expected. In the case of the former child, it is essential that his/her move towards independent 'free-reading' is appropriately scaffolded so that motivation to read turns into a real desire to read; without this, gaps in progress often begin to widen.

As well as accelerating the development of comprehension and the acquisition of vocabulary and grammar, genuine independent reading is linked to the development of positive learning habits, including those of absorbed concentration, curiosity and resilience. The benefits of reading for pleasure include: 'positive reading attitudes, pleasure in reading in later life and increased general knowledge' (Clark and Rumbold, 2006).[4]

[1/2/3/4] Education Standards Research Team, *Research evidence on reading for pleasure*, May 2012.

In early KS2, a child's perception of him/herself as a reader can become cemented, so it is vital that everything that can be done to encourage him/her into true independence is done. Class teachers will be familiar with the tendency for parental involvement with reading to decline as children progress through KS2, making the need for independence and self-reliance all the more pressing. Added to this, it is often at this pre-pubescent stage that a child visibly demonstrates a conscious desire for independence without adult intervention.

Independent readers read for purpose as well as for pleasure, and this is crucial to their ability to drive their own cross-curricular learning. The new National Curriculum, in its introduction to the English Programmes of Study, states the undeniable truth that, 'It is essential that, by the end of their primary education, all pupils are able to read fluently, and with confidence, in any subject in their forthcoming secondary education'. The same introduction also says, 'Reading widely and often increases pupils' understanding and vocabulary because they encounter words they would rarely hear or use in everyday speech. Reading also feeds pupils' imagination and opens up a treasure-house of wonder and joy for curious young minds.' It is this more than anything that might motivate us in the tricky business of creating truly independent readers.

Creating a whole-school culture of independent reading

First and foremost, it is worth remembering that learning almost always begins with imitation. We are probably all aware that children who see their parents or carers read for pleasure and/or for a purpose are more likely to become 'real' readers than those who never experience this. Given this fact of learning, it becomes crucial that children see adults reading: reading to children, yes; but also catching adults reading to themselves, and hearing adults talking about reading for pleasure and purpose. Try, if you can, to have visiting adults be 'caught reading' (even if there is an element of staging involved!): the impact on many boys, who may never have seen a man reading, of catching a visiting male police or fire officer, or football coach, reading to himself, can be profound.

Additionally, the whole-school culture can celebrate reading and books overtly through such simple measures as favourite book assemblies, staff displays of best books, and signs on classroom doors to the tune of, 'Mrs Smith is currently reading _____.'

There is so much else that schools do to build a culture of independent reading; you will be familiar with many of the ideas that follow, but there may be some new ideas to try.

Book displays

It goes without saying that having lovely texts well-displayed and readily accessible is vital. Availability of the best possible range of high-quality texts can be enhanced by sorting and sifting regularly: it is not unknown for children to become newly excited by existing library stock simply because the older, tattier material has been removed, and over-stuffed shelves and picture-book boxes can be a physical challenge to young hands.

While it may not be possible to replicate the environments of successful bookshops, take inspiration from them nonetheless: loosely-filled shelves, 'face out' displays of newer and more popular titles, recommendations on 'belly-bands' (the strips of paper staff wrap around books to celebrate their favourite reads). And take an honest look at your reading environment: even the loveliest, most comfortable ones can lack 'boy appeal'. Have children design reading areas – make it a cross-curricular project, involving measurement and costing – and then vote on and work from the best design, ensuring a feeling of ownership and involvement.

Reading at the heart of planning

Plan for texts to be at the centre of all learning – have reading at the heart of medium-term planning. Make sure that children experience the purposeful aspect of reading. Having a need to find something out makes reading a means to an end rather than the end in itself.

Five minutes a day

Make time for reading to the class every day, even if it is only 5 minutes. Children *need* to be read to – there really is no better way of engendering a love of story, while also exposing them to wonderful words and worlds – particularly as busy lives prevent many parents from doing this. When you are particularly short for time, try reading in 60 and 90 second bursts through the day: this can leave children begging for more. But also keep reminding yourself that *this is important*. Education is *not* like medicine: it doesn't have to be unpleasant to be working!

Book clubs

Run high-status book clubs (perhaps involving refreshments), and encourage boys and girls perceived as 'cool' to join. Ensure there is a great deal of choice involved; taking a group of six targeted children to a bookshop and helping them select one or two group texts can be a relatively cheap but extremely effective way of instigating a successful club – some schools have used a little Pupil Premium money for this. Once the club is up and running, allow members to promote books with other children through any methods they prefer: posters, assemblies, word-of-mouth.

> Above all, every member of staff has to be committed to the idea that *enjoying* reading is crucial. If we can help children genuinely to love reading, most of what we want to achieve in Primary education falls into place.

Independent reading in the classroom

Once an exciting context for classroom learning is communicated, the vast majority of junior-aged children will be motivated to read. However, most teachers will also have encountered those who avoid reading, apparently at all costs: changing books numerous times within a short space of time and finding distractions from the intended activity. Having high-quality texts from which to choose is only part of the solution: creating a desire to read is paramount.

Tips for encouraging excitement around independent reading

Choice

- Timetable daily (or frequent) 'choice' reading, but try not to assume that merely instructing children to read will work: besides having high-quality texts available, there may be a need to model and nurture the ability to choose texts, as some children have limited experience in choosing freely.
- Value independently-chosen texts, whatever they may be – even the umpteenth book about princess fairies or dinosaurs. Always remember that enjoyment of reading is key, and that when we want to enjoy reading, seldom would we choose on the basis of how far a book stretches decoding or comprehension skills. Often, pleasure in reading is about cosiness, familiarity and even repetition. Never tell a child that a free-choice book is too easy or too hard: it is their choice. Many able readers choose to read easy material, and many people become readers by struggling through something that is tough but that they want to read. Similarly, it is absolutely fine to reread a text, over and over – in fact, this behaviour often marks out a child (and many an adult) as someone who loves reading.
- Make the experience sociable: set up unsupported group reading. Allow children to choose the reading material, and make the choice broad – from comics and magazines to leaflets for theme parks, popular project texts, web-based information or even audio-only. Let children generate their own discussions and questions, and try not to interfere. (One thing to remember is that it is hard for groups to manage themselves when there are more than four people involved; threes often work best.) An element of responsibility, such as putting a short presentation together, can help to focus minds, but may not be necessary.

Cross-curricular opportunities

In a humanities or science lesson, make different children (or groups of children) responsible for different areas of learning: they must find information and share it; the others are depending on it!

Purposeful reading

Include purposeful reading in pleasurable and reward-based activities ('golden time' and similar). For example, have instructional texts that lead towards desirable and shareable end-goals, such as performing magic tricks or making exciting paper aeroplanes.

Showing an interest

Talk with children about their reading and show interest in whatever it may be. This may involve listening to long descriptions of superheroes or types of spaceship, but this is independent reading, and the discussion is about their comprehension. Wherever possible, prompt children to share their interest and learning with peers. Tapping into children's interests can open up a wealth of independent research and communication opportunities, especially where these develop into personal mini-projects.

Audio books

Audio books can be used in a number of ways to promote enjoyment of reading. Using these alongside the printed text can be an effective way of motivating children to read, and many children enjoy 'reading along'. But simply listening is also valid, and is similar to being read-to by an adult. Some children enjoy the shared experience of listening to a story in a group, but others may like to close their eyes on their own and enjoy the images evoked in their heads. Making audio books accessible at home (via CDs or downloads) should be a priority in the absence of an available adult, and where English is an additional language. Additionally, and to further increase exposure to wonderful stories, you might have audio books playing during registration and changing for PE (often a good way of achieving quiet, if the story is engaging enough) and imitate the practice of many artists by listening to an absorbing read while creating a masterpiece.

Rewarding achievement

- Celebrate moves towards independence and make sure that targets for achieving independent reading are the norm. Give specific praise around absorption, enthusiastically talk about texts and make real recommendations to other children.

- We might balk at bribery for reading – it should be a pleasure in its own right – but a reward system (stickers, 'golden time' minutes) linked to quantity read can turn some children into real readers simply by getting them started and keeping them going for long enough to hook them. This can work particularly well if there is a strong series of books or a particular author that a child may become intrigued by. This approach may also help those reluctant readers who find it very hard to persevere through the opening pages or chapter, if it is broken down into chapter-based rewards.

- If a child *successfully* recommends a book to another reader (i.e. the second child reads it and loves it), this act should be considered worthy of the highest level of award: consider real medals, book tokens, celebrity status.

Alternatives to book reviews

- Some children love to write book reviews, but some children abhor having to do this so much that they will avoid ever finishing a book so that they never have to write one. Have alternatives to book reviews to choose from, such as character profiles, wanted posters, key scenes in play script, and making the aforementioned 'belly bands'. And how about an audio or video book recommendation?

- Have children create branching flow charts of book recommendations based on the 'If you liked ____, you will love ____' formula. Let this grow as a display around the walls, and see if different children's branches can link, so that they start looking at texts they might not otherwise have considered.

The Simple View

The *Simple View of Reading* is a very helpful device for thinking about grouping children differently for independent reading tasks.[1]

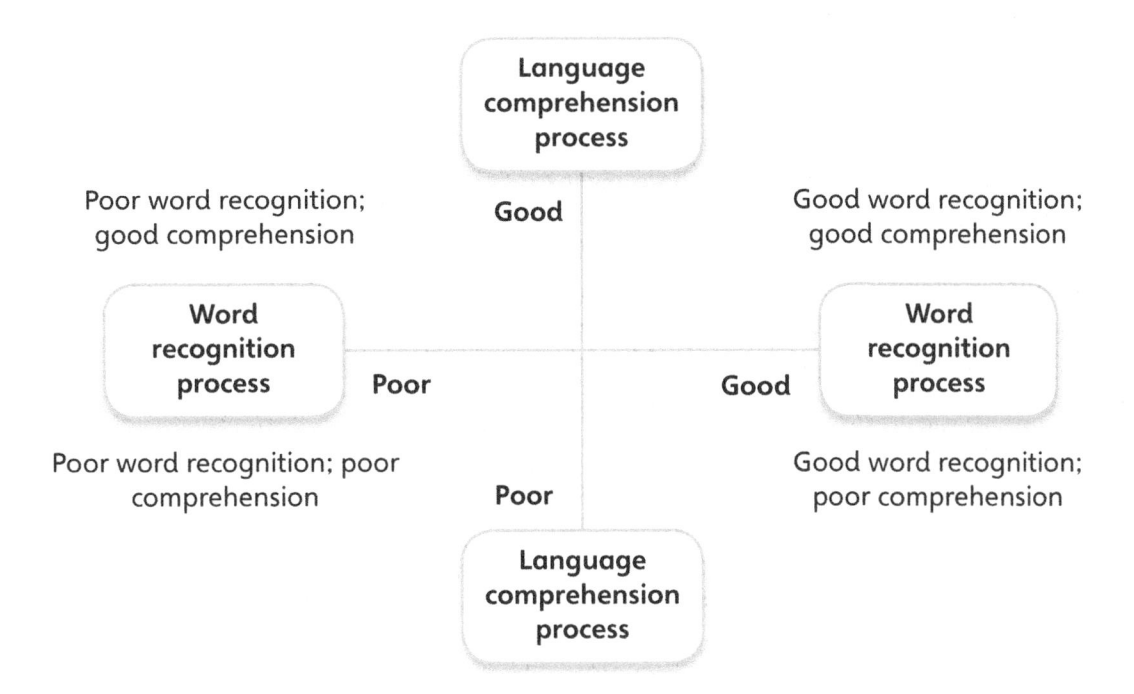

```
                    Language
                  comprehension
                     process

   Poor word recognition;      Good        Good word recognition;
     good comprehension                      good comprehension

        Word                                       Word
     recognition                                recognition
       process          Poor         Good         process

   Poor word recognition;                    Good word recognition;
      poor comprehension       Poor          poor comprehension

                    Language
                  comprehension
                     process
```

There will be some children whose word reading is at least age-appropriate, but their comprehension is weak; there will be other children whose skill-set is the inverse of this. Pairing them up for certain purposeful reading situations, like project research, can work very well indeed as their abilities and 'gaps' are complementary. Meanwhile, the children below age-appropriate expectations in both of these areas might be paired with those at-or-above – the struggling reader will receive peer support, while the able reader benefits from the teaching effect.

Review the use of language

- Be careful with the language used around reading. If we set reading as homework, it is perceived as work. 'Reading at home' and 'reading at school' avoid connotations, largely; the real distinction should be between free-choice reading and teacher-directed reading.

Exciting openers and extracts

- Read great introductions or exciting scenes to the class, and then put the book back in the reading area. This approach is similar to the use of trailers for films and TV programmes, and can be so effective that it may be worth having several copies of the book available.
- The use of extracts from novels is not generally recommended for guided reading, but if you know that a story is particularly addictive, you might do some guided analysis of a key scene and then let the group have the text once they are fully hooked.

---

[1] DfES Publications, *Independent review of the teaching of Early Reading*, © Crown Copyright 2006.

The importance of talk, reading aloud and reading partners

Talk

Like independent reading itself, we all know that children should be encouraged towards independent discussion about text, but simply instructing them to do so very seldom works. Renowned expert on Primary reading and founder of *Write Away*, Nikki Gamble, has developed a wonderfully effective model for systematizing group discussion about text independent of adult support:

Step 1: Every child in a small group reads the same short text (or chapter), making notes on open prompts along the lines of: What do you like? What does it remind you of? What is puzzling? Do you have any unanswered questions?

Step 2: Each child takes a turn running through their notes; no other child is allowed to interrupt – everyone must listen in silence!

Step 3: Once everyone has talked through their notes, the group discuss the text, page-by-page, without any prompts at all. They must not leave a page until every member of the group has agreed to move on.[1]

This structured approach ensures that no individual dominates overly, that everyone gets a say and listens to other views and, so, by the time they return to the text together, discussion is quite free-flowing. (And, as Nikki Gamble points out, if you decide to use this same text the next day with this group, the discussion can come in straight away at a pretty high level.)

Beyond this excellent, powerful approach to text-talk, there are a range of strategies worth applying in any KS2 classroom.

---

[1] For more information on Nikki Gamble, visit: **www.oxfordprimary.co.uk** or **www.justimaginestorycentre.co.uk**.

Tips for talk around independent reading

Setting the context

- Consider playing clips of Radio 4-type programmes in which adults discuss favourite reads. This will help children understand that this is something people do – that some people are paid to do – and it will help them develop a language and style that they may never have encountered otherwise. Remember: language is acquired through imitation!
- Display question stems around the room to immerse the children in the language of book talk. Have them on posters, book marks, key-rings and dice, spinners and even on paper 'fortune tellers'.

Competition and games

- With six children reading the same text, have them work in pairs to generate tough questions (and the answers!) with which to challenge the other pairs. Unanswered questions might contribute to a guided read, or be left in the texts for others to discover.
- In independent text-talk, try issuing 'talk-tokens' (which may simply be counters – three each works well). For every contribution, a child must give a token away; they must also ensure they have no tokens left at the end. If this is challenging at first, consider issuing tokens to pairs within the group.
- Develop on the above by playing 'dialogic Duplo': every child is issued with a set number of the large Lego® bricks (or similar), and each contribution adds to the tower in the middle. The children must decide whether a contribution does actually build on their understanding, or if it is a repetition or an offshoot – with these latter, the bricks are put to one side. Once children have mastered this, it is possible to colour-code different types of response (literal; 'between the lines'; choice of language etc.) with different brick colours.
- Let children read then talk about a text in a time-challenge, similar to Radio 4's 'Just a Minute': can they talk about the text for a set number of seconds without hesitating, 'umming' or repeating themselves? This may need to be adult-led at first, and may involve rehearsal time initially, but children will very quickly be able to work independently, in small groups.

Interviews, role play and presentations

- Have children prepare magazine-style interviews about book recommendations. Let them devise the questions and record the interviews in any way they choose, but they should present the interview in magazine-style, with an appropriate introductory paragraph, and with questions and answers set out like a conversation but without speech marks.
- Use the technique above, but the answers can be given in role, as the author or characters from a story (an extension of the time-honoured hot-seating process). This latter will work particularly well if interviews are timed at different key points within a longer story.
- Have children also prepare for presentations (again, as themselves, the reader, or in role). Offer speaking frames to help structure these, and model the process first. Creating an audio or video recording that can be shared with other classes, other schools or a local library will give real purpose to the process.

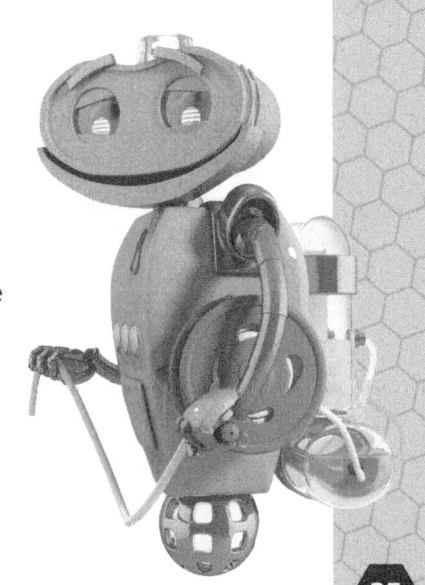

Book groups and discussions

- Create Literary Circles (high-status book groups) or bring independent reading into Guided Reading discussion; encourage small groups to choose a book for discussion so that alternative viewpoints can be explored. This is a great way to overtly value children's choices: every text is worthy of discussion.
- Provide and encourage children to use props to help structure talk around narrative and engage other listeners.
- Have children select a page from the current class story on which to focus their independent discussion. Take feedback on this next time you start class story time. This can help children to spend time thinking about the finer details, such as the language choices made by the author, and to help them to practise the skill of referring to text when justifying opinions. The depth of discussion that can arise from a single page of a high-quality picture book can also lead to some truly inspiring observations and insights.

Emotional learning

- As children read the same text, have them create emotion-graphs independently of each other, plotting a chosen emotion (happiness or worry or fear or excitement, or …) for a chosen character, against time or key events. Ideally, they should note key words and phrases against every peak and trough, as evidence for that particular emotion. Each child's graph then provides a starting point for discussion: did they agree with each other? What about other emotions? Other characters?

Active listening

- Teach active listening skills, such as eye contact, alert posture, showing agreement or otherwise in facial expression. Include prompts for eliciting further thoughts from a speaker: "Go on/Say some more about that/Tell me more about …/How did you know …?/What makes you say …?/Why do you think the author …?/Why do you think he was described as …?/Do you share the same viewpoint?" And crucially, "What is your evidence for that?"

In many of the above suggestions, you might occasionally task particular children (perhaps – but not necessarily – the current high achievers) with monitoring contributions within independent discussion. At the end of any given session, these monitors give feedback on instances where children listened well, contributed usefully, and helped move understanding forward.

Additionally, in many independent group discussions, give children turns at being the teacher – literally. Have them role-play being you, or another teacher in the school, to manage turn-taking and questioning. This sounds risky but almost always produces surprisingly positive results: the children behave well, the experience is simultaneously educational and hilarious, and you might see your own teaching style in a new light!

The importance of reading aloud

If we want children to enjoy reading and to be motivated, independent readers, we need to demonstrate our own enthusiasm for reading. One of the best ways of doing this is to read aloud to them daily. Hearing stories read by adults has a strong impact on children's attitudes towards reading. It helps them develop a positive and long-lasting relationship with books.

> *A particular influence on young children's acquisition of language is the effect of shared book reading with adults. Findings show that early expressive language development was facilitated by joint reading strategies that engaged, supported and promoted children's active participation in the book reading opportunities. The longer a child stayed engaged in the book reading episode, and the more an adult encouraged the child's active participation by expanding on what a child says, or by asking open-ended questions, the greater the effect the reading experience had on the child's language development.*[1]

Modelling fluent expressive reading and encouraging children to respond to what they hear will develop their knowledge of stories, improve their listening skills and extend their vocabulary. Reading aloud enables you to:

- model what 'good reading' sounds like,
- help children to develop the skill of mental imaging by reading, dramatically and with expression,
- nourish their imagination,
- develop their listening skills,
- provide them with an enjoyable experience.

Tips Why not ask volunteers to come in and read? This could mean: dinner supervisors, parents, grandparents or older children within the school. This is not necessarily about reading *with* children, it could be reading *to* children. It's about reading role models and positive reinforcement of the reading experience. It's about having fun with books, rather than teaching reading. However, you may want to provide some support for your volunteers in case the children do want to read to them. For support for volunteers and parents, visit: **www.oxfordowl.co.uk**.

---

[1] Trivette, C. M., Dunst, C. J., Gorman, E., 'Effects of parent-mediated joint book reading on the early language development of toddlers and pre-schoolers'. *Centre for Early Literacy Learning (CELL) Reviews* (2010), 3(2):1–15.

Reading partners

Opportunities to read to and with a reading partner at a similar reading ability can encourage children to share their success as a reader and undertake joint problem-solving when they encounter difficulties. As the 'listener' has to follow the text as well, they too are practising their reading skills.

Reading partners should be encouraged to discuss the books they share: what they thought of them, what they learned and any questions they have. This will help build a culture in which children see reading as a social and pleasurable activity. You could also encourage reading partners to share some of their discussion with the rest of the class.

You will need to model reading partner practice and talk through the prompt sheet opposite. Children could have a copy of the prompt sheet to add their own ticks, or you could enlarge it to A3 poster size and display it in the reading area.

Reading partner prompt sheet

Before reading

Reader and listener:

- Look at the book together.
- What do you think it will be about?

During reading

Listener:

- Listen hard.
- Help your partner if they get stuck on a word.

After reading

Reader and listener:

- Did you like the book?
- Can you say why or why not?

Listener:

Tell your partner what you liked about their reading.

- Did they read with expression?
- Did they 'have a go' at hard words?

Reader and listener:

Decide if the reading was …

- Fantastic
- Good
- A good try but need to read it again.

Independent reading and comprehension at Year 3–4/P4–5

One of the overarching aims for English in the National Curriculum is to ensure that pupils 'read easily, fluently and with good understanding'. Building children's comprehension skills is given a high priority in **Project X *Alien Adventures***. Understanding what has been read is central to being an effective reader and to enjoying reading. Comprehension is not something that comes automatically. The latest research shows that children can be helped to develop comprehension skills by the explicit teaching of certain aspects of comprehension and by offering children specific strategies to help build these aspects. Over time children develop a repertoire of comprehension strategies that they can use across a range of texts.

One aspect of comprehension that struggling readers often find particularly challenging is the ability to close a book and then recap or recount what has just happened or what they have just learned. Memory is crucial to comprehension (and all learning, of course) and we need to help children develop better recall through practice. (Of course, one key reason that struggling readers find recap hard is that their functional, conscious memory has been over-burdened with the basic skills of word reading, and it should go without saying that a child who struggles with these lower-order skills must be actively supported to catch up.)

When reading one-to-one with a child, try the following: keep the word-reading aspect fairly brief, especially if the child is struggling; then have them reread everything they have just read aloud, but to themselves this time. Once they have finished, have them close the book and tell you everything they can remember (and let them return to the text if they get stuck). Notice the chronology of the recount, any gaps, and any misconceptions.

> **Project X CODE** is an innovative reading intervention programme for SEN and struggling readers that's proven to work. Developed with leading experts, it combines systematic synthetic phonics, comprehension, 3D illustration, and a gripping adventure story designed to accelerate children's progress. Find out more about **Project X CODE** at www.oxfordprimary.co.uk.

In order to practise the power of recap and develop memory while reading, we need children to work on the process independently. Task a small group (three may be best) with reading the same text (or part thereof) and then closing it and recounting together. This can be competitive or collaborative, depending on the characters involved. They may record in some way – a mixture of notes and pictures – and then try to build on this with successive revisits to the text. They may try to record recaps using an audio device, so they can hear how they get better over time. And they should always be helped and encouraged to reflect on what helps them remember, in order to better develop their comprehension processes.

Besides this base-level of comprehension, many of the strategies and ideas in earlier sections lend themselves to the development of understanding, particularly those around independent text-talk: the question stems, dialogic-Duplo, emotions graphs and so on mentioned earlier.

Tips for developing independent comprehension

- Generating new (possibly better) titles for books or chapters is an economical and effective method for both developing and assessing understanding. A title is a summary in its purest and most reduced form: doing this effectively is truly a higher-order skill. It is possible to extend the technique to subheadings/subtitles for pages, even for individual paragraphs; where appropriate, these subtitles could be brought to a guided reading session for consideration and discussion.
- In the exploration of a key scene, have pairs or threes plot a dramatic freeze-frame as if they were directors: how would they instruct actors to stand, position their eyebrows, lips, noses? Where and how should the actors be looking? Should they stand close together? … and so on. Make sure these directors have the opportunity to try out their instructions, and have the class assess whether the forthcoming freeze-frame accurately represents the scene just read. (This final phase may have the added benefit of 'selling' the text to other readers.)
- During independent reading, set a timer (old-style sand, or interactive whiteboard version) for around three–five minute intervals, and give children strips of paper that show storyboard-type grids of four or six squares. When the interval is up, children have 10–30 seconds to sum-up, using the grid, what has just happened/what they have just learned in notes, pictures or a combination of both, then the next interval begins. Select children at random to share their 'comprehension grid' with the class, using it to recount the story/their learning.
- The addition of speech and thought bubbles to text illustrations that lack these features is, like the addition of subheadings, a good way to develop and assess comprehension simultaneously. It may be possible, in the difference between the content of speech and thought, to see the development of literal to inferential understanding of characters. Similarly, when exploring play scripts, the formation of thought bubbles in the margins can be an effective way of thought-tracking characters.

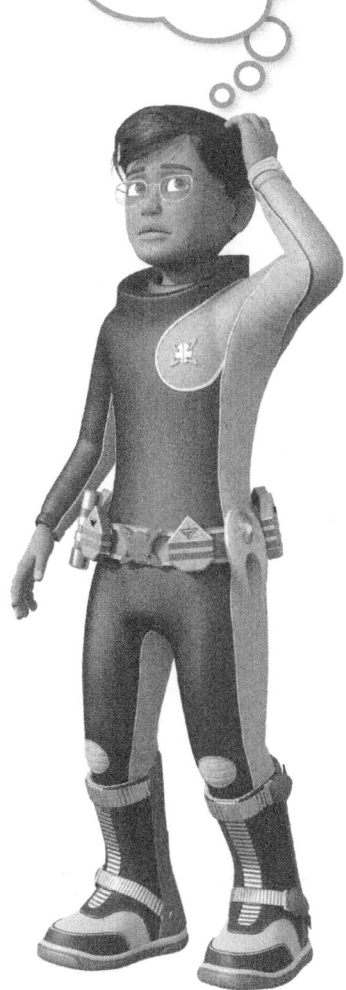

- Something that is often left out of reading comprehension until formal assessment is comparison. Get children weighing up the relative effectiveness of two texts that are working to the same purpose, and have them give reasons for preferences. Comparisons of different titles by the same author or versions of the same story will also enable higher-order analysis.
- Literal understanding is often at the easy end of the comprehension spectrum, but recasting knowledge gleaned from text is something many children need to practise and a skill required in real-life tasks beyond the school gates. Tasking children with using their reading to label a diagram, for example, or to complete a graph or table, stretches application of understanding while encouraging reading for purpose, especially if done in cross-curricular contexts.
- Reading information for the purpose of teaching others has been mentioned earlier, but it bears repeating. Try using 'jigsawing': put children into small groups, and allocate each group member with a number, 1, 2, 3 or 4, so that every group has all the numbers. Then allocate an area of research to each group, that no other group will be studying. Once the brief study time is up, 'jigsaw' the groups: all the 1s come together, all the 2s, and so on; there should now be a representative of each area of expertise in each cluster. The children then take turns to teach the rest what they have learnt. Once completed, children return to their smaller original groups and piece together everything that they have now learned.

The interdependence of reading and writing

The most able writers in a Primary school are almost always enthusiastic, independent readers. The language and the grammar of writing is distinct from that of speech, and children who read for pleasure read so often that they have a sense and a feeling for how writing should sound. It is possible to teach accurate and appropriate written grammar to adequate-but-unenthusiastic readers, but their sentences can seem artificial and seldom cohere into a really effective text. Helping children become truly independent readers is crucial to their success as developing writers.

But some avid readers still find the crossover to writing tricky and need to be prompted. The simple question, 'What have you picked up that you can use in your own writing?' at the end of a guided reading session can help with this transition, as can a focus on author's choice of language: 'How do the verbs help us understand how he is feeling?'

Moving this process into independent reading, giving children a 'writers' journal' or 'magpie book' (a highly effective concept expounded by Pie Corbett) for recording words or phrases that they wish to use in their own writing is popular with children and very useful for language acquisition. Some children benefit from having this as a personal target: 'Use one new word or phrase from your reading, every week in your writing.' This can lead to vital discussion around making appropriate language choices to suit the purpose, audience, style and tone of a text.

At a text – rather than word or sentence – level, you might ask children to detect the viewpoint and themes by getting them to search for the 'golden thread' that runs through a story or piece of information, and then apply this process to their own writing: decide on what viewpoint to take at the planning stage of writing, and then refer back to this repeatedly during the process of writing to achieve cohesion. The 'golden thread' is found by piecing together the specific language choices, emphasis and balance of a piece of writing, and how titles and sub titles are worded can provide clues to the author's intent. This lends itself particularly well to persuasive, discursive and information texts and will support the achievement of writing fluency as well as inference.

The interdependence of reading and writing

Support the analysis of 'how writing hangs together' through the practice of 'reverse planning': turning a story or other text into the plan for itself, reverse-engineering it (in the form of key events or information) on to a story mountain, a flow chart, timeline or other graphic organizer. Seeing how an existing text might have looked at the planning stage can help children understand what planning writing is all about, and therefore how texts are organized.

Consider also that when a child is applying new skills gleaned from reading into his/her own writing, there is a strong element of risk involved, and those children who do not experience success in writing regularly may feel very exposed. Offering opportunities, for example in free-choice writing books or personal writing journals, to write what they like, taking risks, and sometimes even choosing whether or not the teacher marks it, can be very effective for those children who have already labelled themselves as non-writers.

A variation of this that children particularly enjoy is the ownership of a personal portfolio of writing in which children generate 10 titles, and over the course of the year, they draft and develop their own work, often taking inspiration from recent, favourite reads and allowing for sharing with peers, either during the drafting stage or upon 'publication' of the final version.

Partnership with parents and carers

Parental partnership must be part of a whole-school strategy if it is to be effective in improving outcomes for children. Schools should seek to build a relationship of trust between the school and the home that will lead to effective communication.

Research has identified that the quality of the home learning environment has a massive impact on children's progress.

- *Parental involvement in a child's literacy has been reported as a more powerful force than other family background variables, such as social class, family size and level of parental education.* (Flouri and Buchanan, 2004; cited in Clark and Rumbold, 2006).[1]
- *Parents and the home environment are essential to the early teaching of reading and fostering a love of reading; children are more likely to continue to be readers in homes where books and reading are valued.* (Clark and Rumbold, 2006).[2]

When parents/carers and practitioners work together, the results have a positive impact on children's development and learning at home and at school. Washbrook and Waldfogel found that children from poorer backgrounds lag behind their more privileged peers in terms of cognitive development; they also found that activities such as reading to children and having fixed bed times can significantly reduce this gap.[3]

[1,2] Education Standards Research Team, *Research evidence on reading for pleasure*, May 2012.
[3] Washbrook, E. and Waldfogel, J., The Sutton Trust *Low income and early cognitive development in the UK*, (2010).

Partnership with parents and carers

In 2009, Estyn reported that schools which effectively involve parents in supporting children improved standards of achievement: offer flexible arrangements for parents' evenings; provide translators for parents who do not speak English; provide parents with clear information about their expectations regarding the homework policy and set appropriate homework with enough information so that parents know how to help; provide parents with a topic or subject sheet outlining the term's work and choose topics where parents could help easily; record stories for parents who do not speak English to follow the book with their child at home; and encourage parents to borrow 'story sacks' to use at home with their children.[1]

Tips

Here are some ways to encourage parents/carers to get involved with their children's reading.

- Share research with parents/carers that shows children who are read to do better in school.
- Invite parents/carers to a meeting about how you teach reading. As part of the event have a professional storyteller tell a story to encourage parents/carers to tell stories about everyday life to their children.
- Invite parents/carers to participate in a guided reading session in school.
- Encourage parents/carers to look at words in the home and out and about, for example, at breakfast time on cereal packets, milk and fruit juice cartons. When in the car or walking, look at advertising posters, supermarket names and place names. Can children read the words?
- Involve parents/carers in running a book exchange of children's and adult books.
- Encourage parents/carers to read books, newspapers and magazines around the home. Use the slogan 'Read by example'. Ask parents/carers to bring in photographs of themselves reading and display them in the school with appropriate captions.
- Suggest parents/carers provide children with books, comics and writing materials in their bedrooms to encourage children to read and write for pleasure. (On page 38, a photocopiable door hanger has been provided for children to cut out and colour in.)
- Provide parents/carers with a list of books from a range of authors. Regularly 'spotlight' a book in an area to which parents have access.
- Encourage parents/carers and children to join the local library.

Opposite, you will find a sheet of simple tips and practical advice for parents/carers on how to support their child with their reading. This can be photocopied or adapted for your own Home-School programme.

Oxford OWL

For teachers
Helping you with free eBooks, inspirational resources, advice and support

For parents
Helping your child's learning with free eBooks, essential tips and fun activities

www.oxfordowl.co.uk

---

[1] Estyn, 'Good Practice in Parental Involvement in Primary Schools', *Her Majesty's Inspectorate for Education and Training in Wales: 27.* (2009).

Reading with your child

Here are some simple tips to help you help your child with reading at home.

Enjoy it!

- Make book sharing a fun time that you both enjoy – snuggle up with a book!
- Read old favourites together as well as new books.
- If your child reads to you, or joins in when you are reading to them, show them that you are proud of what they can do.

Make time and space

- Make reading a special part of your day. Try to find a time when you aren't busy doing other things so you can spend 'quality time' reading together – even if it's only for a few minutes.
- Try to find a quiet place away from distractions like the television or the computer.
- Try to find some time every day for reading together – 10 minutes each day is better than a long session once a week.

Be positive

- Give your child lots of praise, encouragement and support when they read to you. Focus on what they did well, not what they did wrong. Even small successes are important.
- Never force your child – if they are reluctant to read you could offer a small reward such as playing a game they enjoy. If they are tired or very reluctant, read to them instead.

Find out what they like to read

- Sometimes we read for pleasure but much of the time we read for a reason. Read lots of different things together – stories, information books, comics, magazines, websites, cereal packets, TV listings – anything you and your child enjoy reading or need to read.
- Let your child make his or her own reading choices sometimes. They need to develop their own personal likes and dislikes. It is OK not to like some books! Don't worry if they choose an 'easy' or favourite book over and over again. This is normal and helps children build their reading confidence and enthusiasm.
- Join the local library and let your child choose from the great range of books on offer.

Talk about it

- Talking about books will help your child become more involved and interested in reading and can help them understand more.
- After you've read a book together – or anything else you choose to read – talk about it. What was it about? How did it make you feel? What did you like or not like about it? What did you learn? Spend some time looking at the pictures and talk about what they tell you. Never cover the pictures while sharing a book.
- You can talk with your child about anything – games, TV programmes, films or other things you do together.

Helping you with free eBooks, inspirational resources, advice and support

Oxford OWL
www.oxfordowl.co.uk

© Oxford University Press 2014. Copying permitted within the purchasing school only.

Please knock! I'm reading.

Alien Adventures

About Project X *Alien Adventures* in Year 3–4/P4–5

The **Project X *Alien Adventures*** books in 3–4/P4–5, Brown–Grey Book Bands (Oxford Levels 9–14) provide the perfect support for young readers.

The stories offer practice and consolidation of their previously learned phonics skills while at the same time offering small steps of challenge to stretch their developing reading skills. The fine levelling, coupled with the grammar and punctuation coverage (suffixes, subordinate clauses, conjunctions, etc.) as outlined in the National Curriculum, along with the vocabulary extension, ensures that children build stamina and fluency, develop confidence and experience reading success.

As well as supporting children's word reading and comprehension skills, **Project X *Alien Adventures*** offers exciting stories, built around the core hooks that all children, but particularly boys, will enjoy: fantastic characters, great plots with plenty of action, gadgets and humour.

Space Vultures, Brown Book Band (Oxford Level 10)

The Rust Monster, Grey Book Band (Oxford Level 13)

What children say about Project X *Alien Adventures* …

> All my friends like Dr Who so I know they will like this.
> Billy, age 6

> It's exciting to read about different planets.
> Lauren, age 7

> It's really fun and you don't know what's going to happen next.
> Richard, age 8

> It's got scary bits, exciting bits and you don't know what's going to happen in the end so you just have to read it. Daisy, age 7

> It's definitely worth reading. It's really different.
> Thomas, age 8

> It's exciting and dramatic.
> Ella, age 8

The Project X characters

Project X is unique because of its continuous character story. Following the adventures of popular characters is widely acknowledged as one of the best ways to hook young children in to reading … and to keep them reading.[1]

Project X *Alien Adventures* features the characters Max, Cat, Ant and Tiger – four ordinary children who have discovered four amazing watches … watches that allow them to shrink! They have many fantastic and action-packed adventures, made all the more extraordinary by their ability to shrink to micro-size.

Max

Cat

Ant

Tiger

Max: heroic, kind and generous, the natural leader of the team.

Cat: clever, determined and adventurous.

Ant: intelligent, good at problem-solving, science mad.

Tiger: impetuous, fun-loving, brave.

The new space adventure!

The micro-friends have a dramatic start to their adventures at Year 3–4/P4–5 when they are beamed aboard the **Destroyer** – a ship belonging to the space villain, **Badlaw**! They are looking for the **king and queen of Exis** (the parents of their new alien friend, **Nok**); but they quickly discover that the royal couple have escaped from Badlaw's clutches. The micro-friends' new mission is to find the king and queen before Badlaw's army of metallic **Krools** does …*

It's not a hopeless quest: the king and queen leave a trail of clues for the micro-friends to follow, and, finally the friends rescue them from one of the mighty storm planets. Together they recover the fifth **fragment** of the **Core of Exis** and return to Planet Exis for the final showdown with Badlaw.

After so many adventures, Max, Cat, Ant and Tiger are feeling homesick. As a parting gift, the king and queen give the micro-friends the micro-ship **Excelsa** and an upgraded, female robot, Eight, to help them get home.

However, Badlaw is out for revenge. He can't have Planet Exis, so he sets his sights on a new planet … Earth. The only problem is, er, he doesn't know the way, so he begins to follow the micro-friends in the Destroyer. In an attempt to lose Badlaw, the Excelsa is accidentally sucked into a wormhole! The micro-friends end up in an entirely new galaxy – the Delta-Zimmer Galaxy.

In order to get home they have to shake off Badlaw and get to the **Waythroo Wormhole** before it collapses.

Nok

King

Badlaw

Queen

*NB: Only the bravest, most honest and determined will succeed on this mission.

[1] Bookfeast survey 2009 – 51% of children cited character as the main reason for choosing a book.

The Books

The **24 Project X *Alien Adventures*** books at Year 3–4/P4–5, Brown–Grey Book Bands are broken down into six sub levels: Oxford Levels 9–14. This fine levelling gives children the chance to practise and consolidate their previously learned phonics skills (through Phases 1 to 6 of *Letters and Sounds*) while at the same time offering small steps of challenge to stretch their developing reading skills. Each level, for example, increases in word extent, builds on grammatical devices, such as fronted adverbials, conjunctions and subordinate clauses, etc and extends vocabulary. All of which help to develop fluency and reading stamina and give children the confidence they need to build that all important reading for pleasure habit.

Battle with Badlaw, Brown Book Band (Oxford Level 11)

Features

You will find the following features in the **Project X *Alien Adventures*** storybooks at Year 3–4/P4–5 that are designed to stimulate talk and increase engagement:

Max's mission log: the mission summary at the start of each story, and the recap of the previous adventure, mean that the **Project X *Alien Adventures*** books can be read in any order as they bring the reader up to speed with what has happened in the adventure so far. They also encourage wider reading as children may want to 'go back' and read the previous adventure.

Fact files: these appear throughout the books at Year 3–4/P4–5; they are non-fiction style information 'screens' that give the readers (and the characters) more information about the aliens and the planets that they encounter in the stories. They are great for generating talk and offer a perfect stimulus for writing activities.

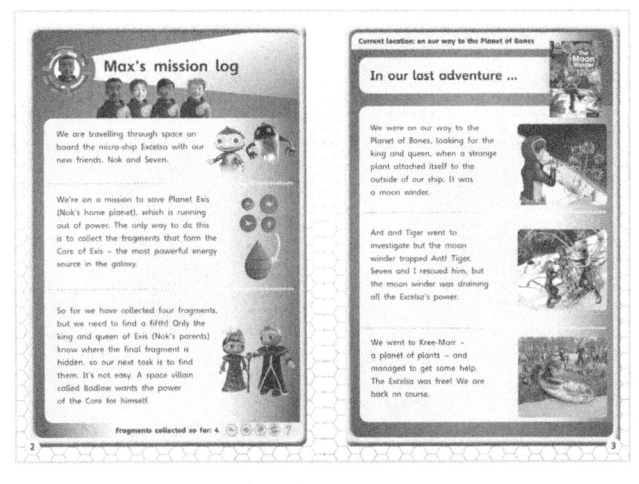

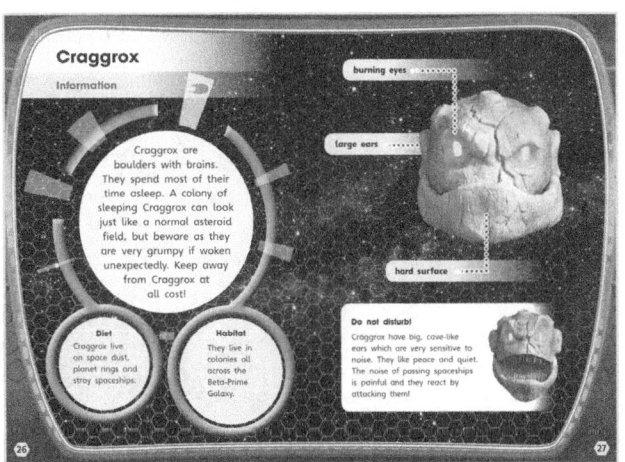

Project X *Alien Adventures* Companion 3

Inspire a love of reading with this children's companion.

Companion 3 is designed to hook children in to the **Project X** *Alien Adventures* series. It gives more information about the special watches, the characters and their spaceships, as well as comic strip adventures, things to make and the *Alien Adventures* game!

How to use Companion 3

The companion can be used by children working on their own, or it can be shared with a friend/s or an adult. It can be used:

- to introduce the **Alien Adventures** series to the whole class and generate excitement about the individual stories before children read them,
- as a springboard for writing opportunities,
- to help generate talk with individuals, groups or with the whole class,
- as a perfect solution for wet breaktimes!

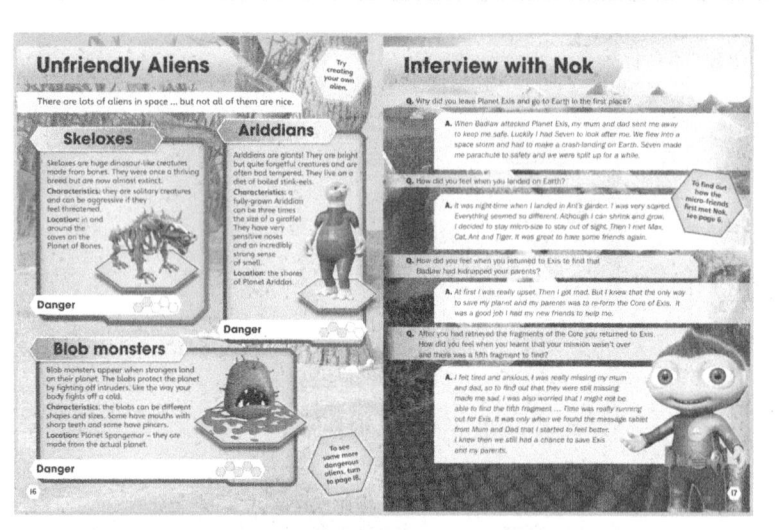

The Project X *Alien Adventures* Companions 1 and 2 eBooks are available free online at www.oxfordprimary.co.uk.

Inside Companion 3 you will find ...

Comic strips: give readers the chance to recap on two key **Project X Alien Adventures** stories: how Max, Cat, Ant and Tiger find Nok's ship – the Excelsa – and blast off into space, and how Badlaw takes his revenge after he is banished from Planet Exis. There is also a new story about how Solon, the nephew of a former king of Exis, tried to steal the Core of Exis! These comic strips are perfect for encouraging talk about characters' feelings.

Questions and prompts: provoke thought and provide opportunities for talk and writing, and **'Find out more'** hexagons inspire further reading and encourage children to explore the companion more deeply.

Character profiles: allow readers to get to know the characters – the goodies and the baddies – in more depth, including their likes and dislikes. You could encourage children to write their own profile.

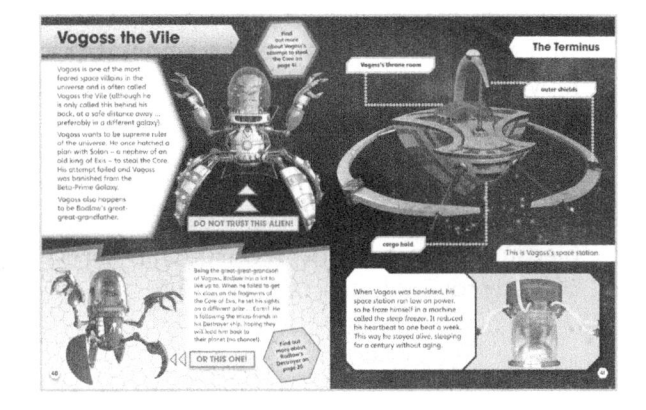

Gadget and vehicle spreads: give readers more information on the special watches, the spacesuits and the spaceships in the series ... perfect for inspiring boys.

Things to make and do: encourage reading for a purpose and for fun.

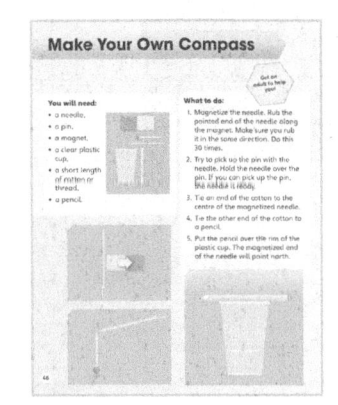

Observation, assessment and planning: Year 3–4/P4–5

Teachers in England will now need to base their assessments on the new National Curriculum Programmes of Study for English. By Lower Key Stage 2 most children should have acquired a wide range of decoding strategies and will be able to read accurately and fluently using their growing knowledge of vocabulary and language structures to support both word reading and comprehension. This is a crucial developmental stage for many children as it is the point at which, having mastered the mechanics of reading, they need to be encouraged to become independent and enthusiastic readers who choose to read often for purpose and pleasure. In order to help children move on from the 'mechanics' to the real purpose of reading, teaching needs to be directed towards developing children's vocabulary and comprehension skills so that they can question and sense-check the meaning in what they read, retrieve information, draw inferences, predict what might happen and justify their views and thoughts.

A swift, well-structured, phonics-based intervention will be needed for those children who are below expectations in word reading for Lower Key Stage 2. **Project X CODE** is the perfect solution for these children as it combines rigorous phonic support with vital motivation and engagement for children whose enthusiasm for reading may already be low. (For more information about **Project X CODE** see www.oxfordprimary.co.uk)

The *Reading Assessment Record* on page 53 will support teachers in assessing individual children against the comprehension and 'reading for pleasure' aspects of the new National Curriculum Programme of Study for English in Years 3 and 4.

The Oxford Ros Wilson Criterion Scale for Reading

Detailed assessment of children's reading progress against the new National Curriculum Programme of Study for English is challenging because the statements of expectation are very broad. This is particularly true at Key Stage 2 where the development of reading skills is less obvious.

Ros Wilson's Reading Criterion Scale is a detailed hierarchy of reading skills divided into seven Grades from Emergent – typically children in the Foundation Stage – through to Grade 6 – typically high-achieving children in Year 6. It is primarily an assessment tool that provides teachers, children and parents with a clear picture of what a child can do and what they need to learn next in order to make progress.

On pages 47–52 you will find extracts from the Reading Criterion Scale for Grades 2 to 4. Most children in Lower Key Stage 2 should be working comfortably within Grade 3 and some will be comfortably within Grade 4 by the time they move up to Year 5.

These Scales can be used termly to assess children's reading using an 'unseen' text at an appropriate level. Through hearing the child read and talking about the book a teacher can observe the skills and strategies a child is using and can make a judgement about how secure each skill is. The 'score' that this assessment process generates will help you identify the Oxford Level a child is most comfortable reading at and it will help you identify the precise next steps of learning for each child.

New

For more information about **Ros Wilson's Reading Criterion Scale** and how the new **Oxford Levels** connect with it go to **www.oxfordprimary.co.uk**.

How to use the Reading Criterion Scale for Assessment

Termly Summative Assessment

Summative assessments can be carried out in small groups or with individual children.

- Organize children into small groups of no more than four and, using your existing knowledge of children's reading, select the Grade on the RCS which is most likely to fit their current reading development. For children in Years 3 and 4, this is most likely to be Grade 2, 3 or 4.
- Photocopy the relevant Grade Criteria chart for each child in the group. For each child, look at the criteria in detail and tick any criteria that you are confident they have already attained. This enables you to focus the assessment on the criteria of which you are more doubtful.
- Prepare for the assessment by selecting a book at the appropriate level – this should be a book which you are confident all the children should be able to read, but which they have not already read. Look at the criteria which you want to focus on in the assessment and use these criteria to prepare questions to ask the children during the assessment.
- Gather the group together and ask them to read part of the chosen book. Sample their reading aloud so that you can assess their word reading skills and then talk to them about their understanding of the text in order to assess their comprehension.
- Against each of the remaining criteria, put a tick if a child has achieved it, a cross if they have not achieved it, and a dot if the child is 'almost there'.
- Count up the number of ticked criteria to work out each child's sub-Grade and the Oxford Level they should be comfortable reading at.
- A child that achieves an 'a' sub-Grade should be assessed for the next Grade up. The letters (AP) mean Assessment Point to flag this up.

Please note: although the criteria in each Grade are set out in broadly hierarchical order, this is only a general guide – children will not necessarily achieve the skills in the order presented – so it is important to consider and assess each criteria on its own merits regardless of where it appears on the Scale.

On-going, formative assessment

You can use individual children's assessments to identify their next steps and plan future teaching. The criteria you marked with a dot are those which children are closest to achieving, so it makes sense to focus on these skills first; the criteria marked with a cross represent the skills which children are furthest from acquiring. It is important to share next steps explicitly with the child so that they know exactly what their targets are and what they need to do to make progress in the short term and over the longer term. Once a child's next short term targets have been agreed you can carry out on-going, formative observation and assessment during guided or independent reading sessions and record evidence of any criteria which are achieved between formal assessments.

Oxford Assessment and Levelling for Reading: The Guide

This new publication provides detailed guidance on Oxford Assessment and Levelling for Reading, including information on the new Oxford Levels, the Reading Criterion Scale Grade Charts for the whole-school (Emergent Grade through to Grade 6) and correlation between Oxford Levels, RCS Grades and the new national curriculum. For more information visit: www.oxfordprimary.co.uk

Oxford Ros Wilson Reading Criterion Scale
Assessment Grade 2

Name: _____ Date: _____

Grade	Oxford Level
Grade 2c	Levels 7 and 8
Grade 2b	Level 9
Grade 2a (AP)	Level 10

Grade 2c: 9–15 Grade 2b: 16–24 Grade 2a (AP): 25–31 and assess for Grade 3	READ skills	✓ ✗ ●
1. Can read most of the Y1–2/P2–3 high-frequency words lists.	Read	
2. Can use phonic strategies when reading unknown words; however, may need support when reading long-vowel phonemes that have several representations (*e.g.* ai, a_e) or graphemes that have more than one sound (*e.g. bread, read, beach*).	Read	
3. Knows the function of full stops when reading and shows this in their reading aloud.	Read	
4. Can retell an unknown story (unfamiliar before first reading) beginning, middle and end (may only be in simple terms because of its unfamiliarity but children have got the general gist of the story as a whole).	R	
5. Can use the front cover, book title as well as illustrations and words inside to make reading choices.	E	
6. Can locate specific information on a given page in response to a direct question.	R	
7. Can relate stories/texts to their own experiences, including story settings and incidents.	D	
8. Can comment on obvious characteristics and actions of characters in stories.	D	
9. Is beginning to distinguish between fiction and non-fiction.	A	
10. Can use a range of phonics strategies to read unknown regular words.	Read	
11. Can identify when reading does not make sense and self-corrects in order for the text to make sense.	Read	
12. Can read aloud, taking into account ? !	Read	
13. Can locate some specific information (*e.g. key events, characters' names etc. or key information on a non-fiction page*).	R	
14. Can make predictions about a text using a range of clues (*e.g. experience of books written by the same author, experience of books already read on a similar theme, book title, cover and blurb*).	D	
15. Can compare similarities and differences between texts/books in terms of characters, settings and themes.	D/E	
16. Can provide simple explanations about events or information (*e.g. why a character acted in a particular way*).	D	
17. Is beginning to talk about the features of certain non-fiction texts (*e.g. non-chronological report, information poster, letter*).	A	
18. Is beginning to use contents and index pages to locate information in non-fiction texts.	A	
19. Can read all of the high frequency words, up to and including the Y1–2/P2–3 high frequency word list (fluent reading of frequently encountered words without 'sounding and blending').	Read	
20. Can use syllables to read unknown polysyllabic words, including knowledge of common prefixes and suffixes (*e.g.* un-*im*-por-tant).	Read	
21. Can read words with contractions (*e.g. I'm, I'll, we'll*) and understand that the apostrophe represents the omitted letter(s).	Read	
22. Can read aloud with intonation, taking into account a wider range of punctuation (. ? ! ,).	Read	
23. Can explain the meaning of 'WOW' words in context (appropriate level of book) (*e.g. despair, marvel (including words with common prefixes and suffixes e.g. undecided, forgetful*)).	D	

© Andrell Education Ltd 2013 published by Oxford University Press. Copying permitted within purchasing school only.

Oxford Ros Wilson Reading Criterion Scale
Assessment Grade 2 (continued)

Grade	Oxford Level
Grade 2c	Levels 7 and 8
Grade 2b	Level 9
Grade 2a (AP)	Level 10

Name: _____ Date: _____

Grade 2c: 9–15 Grade 2b: 16–24 Grade 2a (AP): 25–31 and assess for Grade 3	READ skills	✔ ✘ ●
24. Can summarize a story, giving the main points clearly in sequence.	R	
25. Having read a text (level appropriate), can find the answers to questions, both written and oral.	R	
26. Can talk about how different words and phrases affect meaning.	E	
27. Can discuss reasons for events in stories by beginning to use clues in the story.	D	
28. Is beginning to read between the lines, using clues from text and pictures, to discuss thoughts, feelings and actions.	D	
29. Can talk about the features of certain non-fiction texts (non-chronological report, recount, letter).	A	
30. Can demonstrate how to use information books (by using layout, index, contents page, glossary).	A	
31. Can ask questions before reading a non-fiction text and look for the answers within the text when reading.	R	

Key

READ skills	Meaning	✔ ✘ ●
Read	The 'Read' skill focuses on the mechanics of reading – phonics and decoding, sight words, and reading aloud.	Put a tick if a child has achieved the criteria, a cross if they have not achieved it, and a dot if the child is 'almost there'.
R	The 'R' stands for RETRIEVE. This skill relates to retrieving information directly from the text (often referred to as 'literal comprehension').	
E	The 'E' stands for EXPLORE, and it focuses on the author's use of language.	
A	The 'A' stands for ANALYSE. Here we ask children to analyse the structure, organization and presentational features of texts.	
D	The 'D' stands for DEDUCE and INFER. This skill relates to locating information in texts and reading between the lines.	

© Andrell Education Ltd 2013 published by Oxford University Press. Copying permitted within purchasing school only.

Oxford Ros Wilson Reading Criterion Scale
Assessment Grade 3

Name: _____ Date: _____

Grade	Oxford Level
Grade 3c	Level 11 and 12
Grade 3b	Level 13
Grade 3a (AP)	Level 14

Grade 3c: 8–15 Grade 3b: 16–22 Grade 3a (AP): 23–29 and assess for Grade 4	READ skills	✓ ✗ ●
1. Can read independently using a range of strategies appropriately, including decoding, to establish meaning.	Read	
2. Can read aloud with expression and intonation taking into account . ? , ! as well as inverted commas ("") for dialogue.	Read	
3. Can summarize and explain the main points in a text, referring back to the text to support this.	R	
4. Can explore some straightforward underlying themes and ideas (those that are not clearly signalled at a literal level) in an appropriate level text.	D	
5. Can make plausible predictions based on knowledge from/of the text and wider connections (*e.g. other books on same theme; other books by same author; a personal connection the child makes; a connection the child makes to wider experiences*).	D	
6. Can explain how and why main characters act in a story, using evidence from the text.	D	
7. Can make choices about which texts to read based on, and referring back to, prior reading experience, expressing preferences and comparing texts.	E	
8. Understands the purpose of a paragraph/chapter (the way in which writers use paragraphs and chapters to group related ideas together).	A	
9. Identifies where language is used to create mood, build tension or paint a picture.	E	
10. Can use knowledge of the alphabet to locate information (*e.g. dictionary, index*).	A	
11. Can read most Y4–5/P5–6 high-frequency words.	Read	
12. Is able to quote directly from the text to support thoughts and discussions.	R	
13. Can discuss reasons for actions and events based on evidence in the text.	D	
14. Can discuss how characters are built from small details.	D	
15. Can explore potential meanings of ambitious vocabulary read in context, using knowledge of etymology (the word origin), morphology (the form and structure of a word, i.e. the 'root' word plus prefix and/or suffix), or the context of the word.	D	
16. Sometimes empathizes with different characters' points of view in order to explain what characters are thinking/feeling and the way they act.	D	
17. Can comment on the author's choice of language to create mood and build tension.	E	
18. Can identify the differences between a wider range of non-fiction text types (*e.g. instructions, explanations*).	A	
19. Can identify language features of some different text types (*e.g. that the language of recount is different from the language of instructions*).	E	
20. Can read all Y4–5/P5–6 high frequency words.	Read	
21. Can read aloud with intonation and expression, taking into account higher level punctuation, including … ( ) - .	Read	
22. Can locate information by skimming (for a general impression) and scanning (to locate specific information).	R	

© Andrell Education Ltd 2013 published by Oxford University Press. Copying permitted within purchasing school only.

Oxford Ros Wilson Reading Criterion Scale
Assessment Grade 3 (continued)

Grade	Oxford Level
Grade 3c	Level 11 and 12
Grade 3b	Level 13
Grade 3a (AP)	Level 14

Name: _____ Date: _____

Grade 3c: 8–15 Grade 3b: 16–22 Grade 3a (AP): 23–29 and assess for Grade 4	READ skills	✔ ✘ ●
23. Can use text marking to support retrieval of information or ideas from texts (*e.g. highlighting, notes in the margin*).	R	
24. Can recognize how a character is presented in different ways and respond to this with reference to the text.	D	
25. When prompted, can justify and elaborate on opinions and predictions, referring back to the text for evidence.	D	
26. Is beginning to distinguish between fact and opinion in texts.	E	
27. Can use clues from action, description and dialogue to establish meaning.	D	
28. Is beginning to identify differences between different fiction genres.	A	
29. Is beginning to read between the lines to interpret meaning and/or explain what characters are thinking/feeling and the way they act.	D	

Key

READ skills	Meaning	✔ ✘ ●
Read	The 'Read' skill focuses on the mechanics of reading – phonics and decoding, sight words, and reading aloud.	Put a tick if a child has achieved the criteria, a cross if they have not achieved it, and a dot if the child is 'almost there'.
R	The 'R' stands for RETRIEVE. This skill relates to retrieving information directly from the text (often referred to as 'literal comprehension').	
E	The 'E' stands for EXPLORE, and it focuses on the author's use of language.	
A	The 'A' stands for ANALYSE. Here we ask children to analyse the structure, organization and presentational features of texts.	
D	The 'D' stands for DEDUCE and INFER. This skill relates to locating information in texts and reading between the lines.	

© Andrell Education Ltd 2013 published by Oxford University Press. Copying permitted within purchasing school only.

Oxford Ros Wilson Reading Criterion Scale
Assessment Grade 4

Name: _____ Date: _____

Grade	Oxford Level
Grade 4c	Level 15
Grade 4b	Level 16
Grade 4a (AP)	Level 17

Grade 4c: 8–16 Grade 4b: 17–24 Grade 4a (AP): 25–32 and assess for Grade 5	READ skills	✓ ✗ ●
1. Can read a range of level-appropriate texts fluently and accurately.	Read	
2. Can skim and scan to identify key ideas in the text.	R	
3. Can use knowledge of text structure to locate information (*e.g. use appropriate heading and subheading in non-fiction, find relevant paragraph/chapter in fiction*).	R	
4. Can quote directly from the text to answer questions.	R	
5. Can clarify the meanings of ambitious words and/or phrases in context (appropriate levelled book).	D	
6. Can read between the lines, using clues from action, dialogue and description to interpret meaning and/or explain what characters are thinking/feeling and the way they act.	D	
7. Can explore alternatives that could have occurred in texts (*e.g. a different ending*), referring to text to justify their ideas.	D	
8. Can understand and explain different characters' points of view.	D	
9. Can infer meaning, using evidence from the text and wider experiences.	D	
10. Can recognize the different text features within a variety of mixed-genre texts.	A	
11. Can identify and explain the difference between fact and opinion.	E	
12. Can talk about the effects of different words and phrases to create different images and atmosphere (*e.g. powerful verbs, descriptive adjectives and adverbs*).	E	
13. Can talk about the author's choice of language and its effect on the reader in non-fiction texts (*e.g. 'foul felon' in a newspaper report about a burglary*).	E	
14. Can locate information quickly and effectively from a range of sources by using techniques such as text marking and using indexes.	R	
15. Can refer to the text to: support opinions and predictions; sum up what you find/discuss/think about; make your point/state your thoughts and ideas; find evidence in and/or around the text to support your views.	R	
16. Can identify and discuss the various features of fiction genres (*e.g. science fiction, adventure, mystery etc.*).	A	
17. Can discuss messages, moods, feelings and attitudes using the clues from the text using inference and deduction skills.	D	
18. Can compare the structure of different stories to discover how they differ in pace, build-up, sequence, complication and resolution.	E	
19. Can compare and talk about the structures and features of a range of non-fiction texts.	A	
20. Can identify the ways in which paragraphs are linked (*e.g. use of connecting adverbs, pronouns for character continuation*).	A	
21. Can identify the point of view from which a story is told and how this affects the reader's response (*e.g. author's bias*).	E	
22. Can discuss how an author builds a character through dialogue, action, description.	D	

© Andrell Education Ltd 2013 published by Oxford University Press. Copying permitted within purchasing school only.

Oxford Ros Wilson Reading Criterion Scale
Assessment Grade 4 (continued)

Name: _____ Date: _____

Grade	Oxford Level
Grade 4c	Level 15
Grade 4b	Level 16
Grade 4a (AP)	Level 17

Grade 4c: 8–16 Grade 4b: 17–24 Grade 4a (AP): 25–32 and assess for Grade 5	READ skills	✓ ✗ ●
23. Can identify relationships between characters, explaining the effects this has on the reader (*e.g. how characters behave in different ways as they interact with different people and/or different settings*).	E/D	
24. Can talk with friends about books and listen to others, in order to share book recommendations and widen understanding of the world.	E	
25. In most level-appropriate texts, can discuss how and why the text affects the reader and refer back to the text to back up point of view.	E	
26. Can understand that figurative language creates images.	E	
27. Can read aloud with pace, fluency and expression, taking punctuation and author's intent into account.	Read	
28. Can discuss the work of some established authors and know what is special about their work.	E	
29. Can justify preferences in terms of authors' styles and themes.	E	
30. Can infer and deduce meaning based on evidence drawn from different points in the text.	D	
31. Can talk about how a character could be seen in different ways, depending on how the author chooses to portray them.	D	
32. Can refer to the text to: support opinions and elaborate; sum up what you find/discuss/think about; make your point/state your thoughts and ideas; find evidence in and/or around the text to support your views; clarify your thinking by elaborating on and justifying your views, using additional evidence and linking to wider knowledge/experiences.	R	

Key

READ skills	Meaning	✓ ✗ ●
Read	The 'Read' skill focuses on the mechanics of reading – phonics and decoding, sight words, and reading aloud.	Put a tick if a child has achieved the criteria, a cross if they have not achieved it, and a dot if the child is 'almost there'.
R	The 'R' stands for RETRIEVE. This skill relates to retrieving information directly from the text (often referred to as 'literal comprehension').	
E	The 'E' stands for EXPLORE, and it focuses on the author's use of language.	
A	The 'A' stands for ANALYSE. Here we ask children to analyse the structure, organization and presentational features of texts.	
D	The 'D' stands for DEDUCE and INFER. This skill relates to locating information in texts and reading between the lines.	

© Andrell Education Ltd 2013 published by Oxford University Press. Copying permitted within purchasing school only.

Reading assessment record: Lower Key Stage 2

This chart can be used at any point to assess children's reading skills in line with the requirements of the new English National Curriculum Programmes of Study for English in Lower Key Stage 2.

Name of child:			
Word Reading skills	Secure	Not secure	Comments
Can apply their growing knowledge of root words, prefixes and suffixes both to read aloud and to understand the meaning of new words they meet			
Can read further exception words, noting any unusual spellings			
Comprehension skills			
Can listen to and discuss a wide range of stories			
Can read books that are structured in different ways			
Can use a dictionary to check the meaning of words read			
Can identify themes and conventions in stories			
Can discuss words and phrases that capture the reader's interest and imagination			
Can check that the text makes sense to them, discussing their understanding and explaining the meaning of words in context			
Asks questions to improve their understanding of a text			
Can draw inferences such as inferring characters' thoughts, feelings and motives from their actions			
Can justify inferences with evidence from the text			
Can predict what might happen from details stated and implied			
Can identify and summarize main ideas drawn from more than one paragraph			
Can identify how language, structure and presentation contribute to meaning			
Can retrieve and record information			
Can participate in discussions about books			

Alien Adventures © Oxford University Press 2014. Copying permitted within the purchasing school only.

Project X Alien Adventures: vocabulary, punctuation and grammar: Year 3/P4

The books at Year 3 cover the statutory requirements for grammar and punctuation as outlined in the National Curriculum for England Year 3, English Appendix 2. A selection of examples have been highlighted in the table below.

Book Band	Oxford Level	Title	Vocabulary (challenge and context words) The following words appear on the inside front covers of each book.	Punctuation	Grammar
Brown	9	The Destroyer	acid, teleport, access, stomach, lone, intruder, eerie, beckoning	Introduction to inverted commas to **punctuate** direct speech, e.g. "We must go back down to Exis," cried Nok. "Seven needs help!" (p7)	Formation of **nouns** using a range of prefixes, e.g. *teleport* (p4, p6, p7), *outside* (p11), *micro-ship* (p18).
		Space Rat Rescue	glimpsed, hesitated, scrambled, strange, equipment, definitely, excitedly, examining	Introduction to inverted commas to **punctuate** direct speech, e.g. "Come on!" cried Max. "The rat might show us a way out." (p4)	Use of the **forms** *a* or *an* according to whether the next **word** begins with a **consonant** or a **vowel** e.g. 'A strange-looking rat' (p4), 'an ear-splitting alarm' (p22), 'a hot laser beam' (p28), 'an energy ball' (p27).
		Crunch Time!	thoughtful, concentrate, whirred, chutes, cautiously, sign, cubes, makeshift	Introduction to inverted commas to **punctuate** direct speech, e.g. "Don't worry, Nok," Cat said gently. "We'll find them." (p5)	**Word families** based on common **words**, showing how words are related in form and meaning, e.g. *weak, weakest, faintest, fades* (p7–8).
		The Moon Winder	cautiously, swivelled, host, parasite, maturity, cocoon, nervously, atmosphere	Introduction to inverted commas to **punctuate** direct speech, e.g. "It's got hold of Ant!" Tiger yelled. (p10)	Expressing time, place and cause using **conjunctions** [e.g. *so* (p2, p3, p28), *but* (p10)], **adverbs** [e.g. *then* (p10, p13, p29), *soon* (p32)], or **prepositions** [e.g. *in* (p4, p7, p29, p30), *of* (p9, p10, p12, p16)].
		Space Vultures	meteorite, bulging, completely, aggressive, scavengers, immediately	Introduction to inverted commas to **punctuate** direct speech, e.g. "There's a floating meteorite field ahead," Cat said. "Let's hide in there." (p5)	Headings and subheadings to aid presentation, e.g. p2–3, p4, p12–13.
	10	The Planet of Bones	suspiciously, interfering, circuits, extinct, protective, predators, vegetation, species	Introduction to inverted commas to **punctuate** direct speech, e.g. "There are no signs of life," said Ant. "It doesn't look as if anything could survive here." (p4)	Use of the **present perfect** form of **verbs** instead of the simple past, e.g. 'So far we have collected …' (p2), 'The Krools must have been here …'. (p22).

Project X Alien Adventures: vocabulary, punctuation and grammar: Year 3/P4 (cont.)

Observation, assessment and planning: Year 3–4/P4–5

Book Band	Oxford Level	Title	Vocabulary (challenge and context words) The following words appear on the inside front covers of each book.	Punctuation	Grammar
Brown	10	Starmite Swarm	convert, proved, cruising, emerged, chaos, figured, manually, gnashed	Introduction to inverted commas to **punctuate** direct speech, e.g. 'Ant turned to Nok and Seven. "Have you ever seen anything like this before?" he asked.' (p5)	Introduction to paragraphs as a way to group related material, e.g. p2–3, p10, p18.
		The Giants of Ariddas	accelerate, scurried, insisted, delicate, protesting, droned, circuit, retreat	Introduction to inverted commas to **punctuate** direct speech, e.g. "Uh oh," said Cat suddenly. "I've detected a Krool ship on our tail." (p6)	Formation of **nouns** using a range of **prefixes**, e.g. *micro-friends* (p8), *super-strong* (p13), *inside* (p22), *micro-size* (p29).
		The Craggrox Awake	beacon, stalagmites, eerie, languages, legend, stalactite, melody, asteroid	Introduction to inverted commas to **punctuate** direct speech, e.g. Tiger shuddered. "Scary alien voice alert!" (p6)	Use of the **present perfect** form of **verbs** instead of the simple past, e.g. 'So far we have collected …' (p2), "Have you finished translating …" (p29), "The Sirens have seen my parents …" (p36).
		Attack of the Blobs	impatiently, navigating, emerging, exhausted, fascinated, antibodies, reacting, co-ordinates	Introduction to inverted commas to **punctuate** direct speech, e.g. "I have to go!" Cat argued. "I'm supposed to be navigating to Planet Spongemar …" (p5)	Expressing time, place and cause using **conjunctions** [e.g. *when* (p3, p15), *so* (p2, p45), *but* (p2, p3, p4, p14, p16, p43)], **adverbs** [e.g. *then* (p12, p14, p28, p38), *later* (p46), *soon* (p6)] or **prepositions** [e.g. *over* (p14, p17) *after* (p30), *inside* (p15, p19, p35)].
	11	The Image Maker	mysterious, definitely, deserted, uneasily, malfunction, surrender, illusions, eerily	Introduction to inverted commas to **punctuate** direct speech, e.g. "Wow! I wonder who built that," said Ant, gazing at the city in amazement. (p8)	Headings and subheadings to aid presentation, e.g. p2–3, p4, p6, p25.
		Battle with Badlaw	violent, fierce, despair, materialized, located, doubted, dwindling, submerged	Introduction to inverted commas to **punctuate** direct speech, e.g. "Our best chance is to head for the planet," Max said quickly. (p8)	**Word families** based on common **words**, showing how words are related in form and meaning, e.g. *swirling, strong, storms, violent, dangerous, fierce, battered* (p6–9).

55

Project X Alien Adventures: vocabulary, punctuation and grammar: Year 4/P5

The books at Year 4 cover the statutory requirements for grammar and punctuation as outlined in the National Curriculum for England Year 4, English Appendix 2. A selection of examples have been highlighted in the table below.

Book Band	Oxford Level	Title	Vocabulary (challenge and context words) The following words appear on the inside font covers of each book.	Punctuation	Grammar
Grey	12	Badlaw's Revenge	upgraded, outnumbered, acceptable, conquer, lumbering, unpredictable, immense, precise	Use of inverted commas and other **punctuation** to indicate direct speech, e.g. Ant turned to Eight. "Which parts of the ship have been upgraded?" he asked. (p16)	Standard English forms for **verb inflections** instead of local spoken forms, e.g. "you're going …", "we want to …". (p5), "I didn't realize …". (p6).
		The Rats of Rolia	gashes, lurched, buffeted, motioned, feverish, quarry, menacing, miscalculated	**Apostrophes** to mark plural possession, e.g. 'the Rolians' computer' (p38), 'the Rolians' one great ship' (p46).	The grammatical difference between **plural** and **possessive** –s, e.g. 'the *ship's* voice', 'the *engines* spluttered' (p5), 'one of the *rats* swished its tail, whipping *Tiger's* legs' (p20).
		Trapped in Time	glanced, pulse, engage, directed, various, vent, ports, doubtfully	Use of commas after **fronted adverbials**, e.g. *Immediately,* (p6), *At first glance,* (p11), *The next moment,* (p24), *Just then,* (p30).	**Fronted adverbials**, e.g. *Immediately,* (p6), *At first glance,* (p11), *The next moment,* (p24), *Just then,* (p30).
		Double Cross	surge, cascaded, duties, sternly, assign, manually, brace, sneered	Use of inverted commas and other **punctuation** to indicate direct speech, e.g. "Thank goodness that's over!" exclaimed Max. "Ant, can you give us a damage report?" (p6).	Noun phrases expanded by the addition of modifying adjectives, nouns and preposition phrases, e.g. 'The bridge was full of smoke and the acrid smell of burnt plastic' (p6), 'Seconds later Badlaw's ugly face appeared once more' (p37).
	13	The Rust Monster	regal, vacuumed, magnetic, grimaced, devoured, impatiently, ravenous, evacuate	Use of commas after **fronted adverbials**, *Hundreds of years ago,* (p24), *In no time,* (p32), *Just then,* (p38).	**Fronted adverbials**, e.g. *Hundreds of years ago,* (p24), *In no time,* (p32), *Just then,* (p38).
		Pit-stop Peril	mechanical, detour, diversion, trailing, maintenance, hull, rummaged, restored	Use of inverted commas and other **punctuation** to indicate direct speech, e.g. "*DANGER! Tracer dart within range,*" said the ship.	Use of paragraphs to organise ideas around a theme, e.g. p2–3, p17, p35.

Observation, assessment and planning: Year 3–4/P4–5

Project X *Alien Adventures*: vocabulary, punctuation and grammar: Year 4/P5 (cont.)

Book Band	Oxford Level	Title	Vocabulary (challenge and context words) The following words appear on the inside font covers of each book.	Punctuation	Grammar
Grey	13	The Red Cutlass	entirely, constellation, glared, scrolling, motley, evaporated, winch, sauntered	Apostrophes to mark plural possession, e.g. *The pirates' flag* (p13).	Noun phrases expanded by the addition of modifying adjectives, nouns and preposition phrases, e.g. 'On the main sail was a picture of a skull with a blood-red sword' (p4), 'The first mate, a mean, shark-like pirate called Finflop …' (p5), '… a red-skinned pirate said excitedly' (p6).
		Cyberbee Break Out	wasteland, sabotage, reassuringly, cargo, radiation, stampede, motionless, distress	Use of inverted commas and other punctuation to indicate direct speech, e.g. "Hold on a minute, Tiger," said Ant. "How do we know this isn't one of Badlaw's traps?" (p6)	Appropriate choice of **pronoun** or **noun** within and across **sentences** to aid cohesion and avoid repetition, e.g. 'Cautiously the micro-friends made their way down the holo-ramp. When they were clear of the ship, they each pressed their buttons and grew to normal size …' (p10). 'The boys set off at a brisk pace and, before long, they had left Hestan's ship far behind.' (p22). "Hestan placed them on the control console. "You need to get to the main steering circuits," he said.' (p30).
		Operation Holotanium	wailed, plummeted, stifled, spherical, decisively, malfunctioning, armoured, emerging	Apostrophes to mark plural possession, e.g. *the creatures' short back legs* (p22).	The grammatical difference between **plural** and **possessive** –s, e.g. *the controls for the alarm, the Excelsa's systems* (p6). *As the friends looked on in horror, Badlaw's all-too-familiar voice* (p32), *Tiger's watch, hard clumps* (p45).
	14	An Ancient Enemy	cargo, pelted, propelling, relentless, retorted, decrepit, detours, generator	Use of inverted commas and other punctuation to indicate direct speech, e.g. "Who cares!" said Tiger beside him. "We're lost, we can't find the generator, our friends could be in big trouble, and …" (p26).	Standard English forms for **verb inflections** instead of local spoken forms, e.g. "We're running out … We can't afford …" (p7), "I would guess …" (p12).
		The Fury of Vogoss	surrender, commanded, tyrant, ancient, conquer, sinister, oblivion, century	Use of commas after fronted adverbials, e.g. *A hundred years ago,* (p6), *At that moment,* (p22, p37), *In a flash,* (p23), *In moments,* (p36).	**Fronted adverbials**, e.g. *A hundred years ago,* (p6), *At that moment,* (p22, p37), *In a flash,* (p23), *In moments,* (p36).
		The Waythroo Wormhole	nutrition, generator, lessened, unpredictable, rations, conquer, frantically, dissolve	Apostrophes to mark plural possession, e.g. *To the micro-friends' horror* (p27).	Noun phrases expanded by the addition of modifying adjectives, nouns and preposition phrases, e.g. 'A loud, gurgling noise echoed round the bridge.' (p4), 'A huge, glowing mass of light swirled in front of them.' (p9), 'A tidal wave of goo crashed towards him.' (p21).

Alien Adventures

Certificate for FANTASTIC reading

....

has been awarded this certificate for

....

Project X

Alien Adventures © Oxford University Press 2014. Copying permitted within the purchasing school only.

Alien Adventures

Certificate for FANTASTIC writing

....

has been awarded this certificate for

....

Project X

Project X *Alien Adventures* and the Scottish Curriculum for Excellence

The **Project X** *Alien Adventures* series has been rigorously developed to reflect and support the principles and practice of the Scottish CfE. There is a direct correlation between the advice on teaching literacy developed in **Project X** *Alien Adventures* and in recent guidance from CfE. In particular, the following issues are currently highlighted in Scottish education:

Personalization and choice

The CfE encourages teachers to make professional decisions about the choice and use of teaching resources in their classrooms. **Project X** *Alien Adventures* is designed to be used flexibly, depending upon the needs of pupils and is an exciting addition to the early junior literacy tool kit. Suggestions for innovative ways of using the resource are outlined on pages 10–13.

The CfE stresses the importance of developing the ability to learn independently, encouraging children to set their own personal reading targets and take responsibility for their own learning. As part of the **Project X** *Alien Adventures* resource, there are PD films available online, demonstrating best practice in how to develop independent readers at First and Second Levels. For more information visit: **www.oxfordprimary.co.uk**.

The CfE recommends choice for pupils in the selection of reading books; the **Project X** *Alien Adventures* gives children the opportunity to practise reading phonically-regular and high-frequency words that have been learned previously, using core reading schemes. Young readers already familiar with sight vocabulary and with an understanding of how to use their phonic skills to decode words will enjoy choosing a book from an appropriately colour-coded group of publications. The CfE emphasizes the dynamic sense of power that children experience when they first read a new book without the help of an adult. It is at this turning point in their development that they know and believe that they are 'readers'.

Reading engagement

The CfE recognizes the findings of research, indicating that there is a link between reading success, the enjoyment of books and the number of books that children read. 'Enjoyment', 'motivation', 'exploration' and 'challenge' is key vocabulary in the learning outcomes for reading in the CfE. In Scotland there is concern about how to close the gap in attainment between girls and boys, caused by this lack of engagement in reading and writing among boys. **Project X** *Alien Adventures* books appeal to boys with their colourful, digitally-enhanced pictures, modern themes and exciting stories. Girls and boys connect with the upbeat characters and enjoy the challenge of reading new books and the pleasure of returning, by choice, to the familiarity of old favourites.

Multimedia education

There is an emphasis in the CfE on ensuring that children are exposed to a wide range of different types of text in different media. This multimedia education, which includes teaching and learning about digital and film texts, is referred to as 'future proofing'. The connection between watching stories unfold on screen and reading stories is emphasized through the motivating **Project X** *Alien Adventures* animations, available free, online at: **www.oxfordprimary.co.uk**. The series also uses a modern, 3D digital style in its illustrations. These illustrations increase in complexity and detail as the fantastical world of the space adventure develops.

Celebrating reading success

The CfE emphasizes the development of confident, successful young people and the celebration of effort and success is a feature of school life in Scotland. The certificates (see pages 58–59), bookmarks and other free downloadables accompanying **Project X** *Alien Adventures* will be a welcome addition to school assemblies (for more details visit **www.oxfordprimary.co.uk**).

Young readers who crave detail about the characters, places and gadgets which they read about, will find all this in the motivating companion books that accompany the series (see pages 42–43). A motivating feature introduced at the end of the Primary Two books and bridging into Primary Five, is the addition of 'fact file' spreads, offering detailed information about aliens, new planets and objects of interest. In the middle of the stories, this additional information is written in non-fiction genre with the purpose of elaborating the world of *Alien Adventures* through reports, annotated illustrations, explanations, instructions and even warnings. All children will engage with *Alien Adventures*, but particularly those who already know the four main characters through the **Project X** guided/group reading books (see pages 4–5 for more details or visit **www.oxfordprimary.co.uk**).

Partnerships with parents

Educating parents about the importance of supporting their children's developing literacy is a priority in Scotland. Primary Four/Five teachers will welcome the practical methods suggested in this handbook to encourage parental involvement (see pages 35–38). Also, the clear step-by-step guidance on the inside covers of the children's books, on how to support children's reading, is invaluable for parents. Interesting follow-up activities to teach comprehension are also suggested on inside covers. This advice will enhance the learning experience at home with parent and child and reflects exactly the same advice as that being offered by the Scottish Book Trust and various local authority and government initiatives in Scotland.

Oxford OWL

For teachers
Helping you with free eBooks, inspirational resources, advice and support

For parents
Helping your child's learning with free eBooks, essential tips and fun activities

www.oxfordowl.co.uk

Transitions, active learning and learning through play

Recent CfE guidance focuses on the difficulties that primary pupils experience at the point of transfer from stage to stage in school. A reading resource such as **Project X** *Alien Adventures* helps to bridge different stages and brings coherence to the area of reading. Children welcome well-known characters as they progress from Primary One to the end of Primary Five.

It is in the Brown and Grey Band Books (Oxford Levels 9–14) at P4–5 stages that the style and language of the books heightens to that of 'grand adventure', the style so beloved of children at these stages. Pupils will identify with the young heroes as they assist their alien friend, Nok, to save Planet Exis and defeat the evil Badlaw. As the final Grey Band book draws to an end, with the apparently safe return to Earth of the adventurers, a note of foreboding is struck in the final paragraph, sending a chill down the spine and setting the scene for more adventures to come.

It is an original and exciting idea for children to follow an on-going adventure from Nursery to Primary Five. The serial aspect of the storyline becomes increasingly significant as the thrilling narrative unfolds. The convention of introducing the next book with *Find out what happens next in …* (on the last page of each book) heightens the tension and prepares young readers for the next part in the sequence of the adventure. At P4–5, every book begins with an overview of the story and a summary of the last adventure, cleverly presented as *Max's mission log*. This allows children to skip books if they choose to while keeping abreast of the storyline.

Reading stamina and challenge gradually increase at P4–5, with the number of pages in books rising from 32 to 48 in the middle of Brown Band level and the number of chapters rising from five to eight by the end of Grey Band level. The complexity of sentence construction and vocabulary level gradually become more difficult. Size of print decreases and text becomes increasingly dense. Children are carried along on this journey because the increase in difficulty is almost imperceptible and the level of motivation is so great.

Comprehension

In the area of comprehension, the CfE encourages group discussion of ideas, with children generating their own questions and observations about texts. As with advice on approaches to reading in **Project X *Alien Adventures***, pupils are encouraged to link ideas in reading to their own experience and then to reflect upon and interpret ideas in the text through drama, art and writing, sometimes individually and sometimes in groups.

The active learning recommended by the CfE includes paired reading and various models of reading partnerships. This handbook features practical advice on setting up reading partnerships, alongside ideas for how to train partners and useful resources such as the 'prompt' sheet (see page 29).

Assessment

Formative assessment underpins all learning in classrooms in Scotland and includes peer- and self-assessment for children's learning. Approaches to reading assessment in **Project X *Alien Adventures*** fit well with best practice (see pages 44–57 for more information).

Curriculum for Excellence Literacy and English experiences and outcomes

Primaries Four and Five – first and second levels

Depending on their reading ability, pupils in P4 and P5 will be reading at either first or second level of CfE experiences and outcomes. Brown Band books could be interpreted productively by pupils working at either of these levels but Grey Band books are more appropriate for the most able readers at second level. However it is important to remember that when they are well motivated, our pupils will always surprise us with their determination to learn. Young readers who are keen to progress should be encouraged to do so because the very gradual incremental growth in the level of difficulty from Brown to Grey Band books (Oxford Levels 9–14) is designed to enhance the development of their reading comprehension.

Alien Adventures children's and teachers' publications offer support in delivering the following experiences and outcomes in Reading, Listening and Talking. They also provide a range of follow-up activities to support children's writing.

Year	Oxford Level	Book Band	Project X *Alien Adventures* books	Objectives
Primary 4	9	Brown	• The Destroyer • The Space Rat • Crunch Time! • The Moon Winder	**Reading: first level experiences and outcomes:** • I regularly select and read, listen to or watch texts which I enjoy and find interesting, and I can explain why I prefer certain texts and authors. **LIT 1-11a/LIT 2-11a** • I can use my knowledge of sight vocabulary, phonics, context clues, punctuation and grammar to read with understanding and expression. **ENG 1-12a** • I am learning to select and use strategies and resources before I read, and as I read, to help make the meaning of texts clear. **LIT 1-13a**
	10		• Space Vultures • The Planet of Bones • Starmite Swarm • The Giant of Ariddas	• To show my understanding across different areas of learning, I can identify and consider the purpose and main ideas of a text. **LIT 1-16a** • To show my understanding, I can respond to different kinds of questions and other close reading tasks and I am learning to create some questions of my own. **ENG 1-17a** • I can share my thoughts about structure, characters and/or setting, recognise the writer's message and relate it to my own experiences, and comment on the effective choice of words and other features. **ENG 1-19a**
	11		• The Craggrox Awake • Attack of the Blobs • The Image Maker • Battle with Badlaw	**Reading: second level experiences and outcomes:** • I regularly select and read, listen to or watch texts which I enjoy and find interesting, and I can explain why I prefer certain texts and authors. **LIT 1-11a/LIT 2-11a** • Through developing my knowledge of context clues, punctuation, grammar and layout, I can read unfamiliar texts with increasing fluency, understanding and expression. **ENG 2-12a** • I can select and use a range of strategies and resources before I read, and as I read, to make meaning clear and give reasons for my selection. **LIT 2-13a** • To show my understanding across different areas of learning, I can identify and consider the purpose and main ideas of a text and use supporting detail. **LIT 2-16a** • To show my understanding, I can respond to literal, inferential and evaluative questions and other close reading tasks and can create different kinds of questions of my own. **ENG 2-17a** I can: • discuss structure, characterisation and/or setting, • recognise the relevance of the writer's theme and how this relates to my own and others' experiences, • discuss the writer's style and other features appropriate to genre. **ENG 2-19a** **Listening and Talking: first level experiences and outcomes** • I regularly select and listen to or watch texts which I enjoy and find interesting, and I can explain why I prefer certain sources. **LIT 1-01a/LIT 2-01a** • As I listen or watch, I can identify and discuss the purpose, key words and main ideas of the text, and use this information for a specific purpose. **LIT 1-04a** **Listening and Talking: second level experiences and outcomes** • As I listen or watch, I can identify and discuss the purpose, main ideas and supporting detail contained within the text, and use this information for different purposes. **LIT 2-04a** • As I listen or watch, I can identify and discuss the purpose, main ideas and supporting detail contained within the text, and use this information for different purposes. **LIT 2-04a**

Year	Oxford Level	Book Band	Project X *Alien Adventures* books	Objectives
Primary 5	12	Grey	• Badlaw's Revenge • The Rats of Rolia • Trapped in Time • Double Cross	*Reading: second level experiences and outcomes:* • I regularly select and read, listen to or watch texts which I enjoy and find interesting, and I can explain why I prefer certain texts and authors. **LIT 1–11a/LIT 2–11a** • Through developing my knowledge of context clues, punctuation, grammar and layout, I can read unfamiliar texts with increasing fluency, understanding and expression. **ENG 2–12a** • I can select and use a range of strategies and resources before I read, and as I read, to make meaning clear and give reasons for my selection. **LIT 2–13a** • To show my understanding across different areas of learning, I can identify and consider the purpose and main ideas of a text and use supporting detail. **LIT 2–16a** • To show my understanding, I can respond to literal, inferential and evaluative questions and other close reading tasks and can create different kinds of questions of my own. **ENG 2–17a** I can: • discuss structure, characterisation and/or setting, • recognise the relevance of the writer's theme and how this relates to my own and others' experiences, • discuss the writer's style and other features appropriate to genre. **ENG 2–19a** *Listening and Talking: second level experiences and outcomes* • As I listen or watch, I can identify and discuss the purpose, main ideas and supporting detail contained within the text, and use this information for different purposes. **LIT 2–04a** • As I listen or watch, I can identify and discuss the purpose, main ideas and supporting detail contained within the text, and use this information for different purposes. **LIT 2–04a**
	13		• The Rust Monster • Pit-stop Peril • The Red Cutlass • Cyberbee Break out	
	14		• Operation Holotanium • An Ancient Enemy • The Fury of Vogoss • The Waythroo Wormhole	

Project X *Alien Adventures* and the National Literacy Framework in Wales

The **Project X** *Alien Adventures* series has been developed in line with the Welsh National Literacy and Numeracy Framework (2013). It has also been developed with reference to the National Reading Tests in Year 3 and Year 4.

Progression in literacy

The main aim of the literacy expectations of the Welsh Literacy Framework (2013) is to 'encourage learners to develop and demonstrate their skills in oracy (speaking and listening), reading, and writing for different purposes across the curriculum'. **Project X** *Alien Adventures* aims to support teachers in teaching all three of these aspects with the highly engaging children's books, handbook resources and additional online support materials.

Strand 1 – Oracy across the curriculum

The **Project X** *Alien Adventures* animations and the companion books are perfect for introducing the series in a class session; they can help provoke discussion, build anticipation and generate a 'buzz' around reading independently. For more information on the companions, see pages 42–43, and to watch the animations, visit: **www.oxfordprimary.co.uk**.

The **Project X** *Alien Adventures* series provides support for teachers in developing oracy; as well as the animations and companion books mentioned above, the questions provided on the inside cover notes of each of the books offer plenty of discussion points for adults to use with the children, before and after reading. Furthermore, the *Max's mission log* pages, story recaps and fact file spreads each provide an opportunity to explore new vocabulary and discuss the mission and the places and aliens that the micro-friends visit and encounter.

The stories themselves will encourage children to participate in role play and drama activities as they follow the adventures of the micro-friends. For more information on the importance of encouraging talk and how **Project X** *Alien Adventures* supports speaking and listening, see pages 10–11, 15 and 24–29.

Strand 2 – Reading across the curriculum

At Year 3 and 4, children need to read with maturing fluency, accuracy, understanding and independence. Phonics is an integral part of the reading strategies emphasized in the National Literacy Framework, and, at this level, children need to consolidate their phonological, graphic and grammatical knowledge, together with word recognition and contextual understanding. This should be within a balanced and coherent reading programme.

The **Project X** *Alien Adventures* series offers children a wide range of exciting fiction books to engage children. The stories introduce readers to the core characters – Max, Cat, Ant and Tiger and their new alien friend, Nok. Readers follow these characters as they pursue adventures, face challenges and make choices. Each book in Year 3–4 opens with a *Max's mission log* which provides an opportunity to recap on the mission and on the previous story; this means that children can access these stories at any point in the series: they do not need to read the books in order.

The National Literacy Framework emphasizes the need for children in Year 3 and 4 to be able to use a range of strategies to read including knowledge of phonics, word roots, word families, syntax, text organization and prior knowledge of context. The controlled use of vocabulary in the stories means that children would have also built up a store of high-frequency common words. The children should be able to tackle the longer texts with increasing confidence, independence, and with sustained concentration. There are twelve books at Year 3, Brown Book Bands (Oxford Levels 9–11) and twelve at Year 4 Grey Book Bands (Oxford Levels 12–14). The fine levelling of these books helps children to develop the self-assurance they need to make progress and build their reading stamina and fluency.

In addition, children should be encouraged to read texts aloud and respond to them; they should be able to talk about characters, events, language and information as they predict events and explore meaning. The questions on the inside cover notes of the **Project X** *Alien Adventures* books and the follow-up activities on the Photocopiable Masters (PCMs) in this handbook support the development of these emerging comprehension skills.

There is a particular focus on engaging boys as they continue on their reading journey. The **Project X** *Alien Adventures* books are presented in a 3D digital illustration style – which is particularly appealing to boys (for more information on boys' reading see pages 14–16). There are also a number of stories available in eBook form, which gives children the opportunity to use computer-based materials. For more information visit **www.oxfordprimary.co.uk**.

Strand 3 – Writing across the curriculum

The **Project X** *Alien Adventures* series provides writing opportunities in a number of ways:

- the stories themselves, the mission logs, and the fact file pages act as a perfect stimulus for generating ideas,
- the series companions offer a great springboard for creative writing exercises, both before and after children have read the books,
- the activities mentioned on the inside back cover of each of the books provide opportunities for follow-up work at home or in the classroom,
- the PCMs in this handbook provide extension activities for each of the stories in the series; there are also further PCMs for additional practice.

Literacy Framework Aspect		Year 3	Year 4
		Learners are able to:	Learners are able to:
Strand 1 (Oracy)	Speaking	• explain information and ideas using relevant vocabulary; • organise what they say so that listeners can understand; • speak clearly, varying expression to help listeners;	• organise talk so that different audiences can follow what is being said; • adapt talk showing understanding of the differences between informal talk with friends and more extended talk with a wider group; • explore different situations through role play;
	Collaboration and discussion	• contribute to group discussion, sharing ideas and information.	• contribute to group discussion and help everyone take part.

Literacy Framework Aspect		Year 3 Learners are able to:	Year 4 Learners are able to:
Strand 2 (Reading)	Reading strategies	• use a range of strategies to make meaning from words and sentences, including knowledge of phonics, word roots, word families, syntax, text organisation and prior knowledge of context; • read aloud, using punctuation to aid expression; • use visual clues to enhance understanding;	• use a range of strategies to make meaning from words and sentences, including knowledge of phonics, word roots, word families, syntax, text organisation and prior knowledge of context; • read texts with few visual clues, independently and with concentration; • use understanding of sentence structure and punctuation to make meaning;
	Comprehension	• accurately identify the main ideas and information of a story by linking explicit statements; • take an interest in stories beyond their own experiences;	• accurately identify the main points and supporting information in texts; • deduce connections; • explore information beyond their personal experience;
	Response and analysis	• use information from texts in their discussion or writing; • make links between what they read and what they already know and believe about the topic;	• select and use information and ideas from texts;
Strand 3 (Writing)	Meaning, purposes and readers	• write for different purposes and readers choosing words for variety and interest; • include relevant details, information or observations in their writing; • note down ideas to use in writing • review and improve sections of their work;	• adapt what they write to the purpose and reader, choosing words appropriately; • explain main idea(s) with supporting details, including observations and explanations where relevant; • gather ideas to plan writing; • improve writing, checking for clarity and organisation;
	Structure and organisation	• use a basic structure for writing; • use visual information if relevant;	• organise writing into logical sequences or sections by beginning to use paragraphs; • use visual information;
	Language	• use language appropriate to writing; • use vocabulary related to the topic or subject context.	• use language appropriate to writing; • use subject-specific vocabulary independently.

Assessment of reading skills

Progress of children in Year 3 and 4 in reading is now assessed in line with the Literacy Framework 2013 and the NRT (National Reading Test), which has now replaced other reading tests in Wales.

Children are required to read a text and answer the associated questions. This text can be downloaded and used with learners in class – either as printed copies or electronically, for example, on an interactive whiteboard. Use of all the **Project X *Alien Adventures*** would enhance comprehension skills in reading, as mentioned above, and could be used as the perfect practice for text/questioning exercises.

For further information on the NLF and the NRT see www.learning.wales.gov.uk.

Project X *Alien Adventures* and the Northern Ireland Curriculum

Project X *Alien Adventures* supports the aims and objectives of the Northern Ireland Curriculum for Literacy and Language in Key Stages 1 and 2, and the development of key skills and capabilities.

Encouraging a disposition to read

Project X *Alien Adventures* features engaging 3D digital illustrations, which children love, and exciting character-based stories to help you to provide a rich literacy environment in which children can choose appropriate stories, experience books independently and foster a disposition towards reading from the earliest stage.

Independent reading

Alongside modelled, shared and guided reading undertaken in Key Stages 1 and 2, **Project X *Alien Adventures*** provides the perfect support for children developing into confident, independent readers. These highly-motivating and finely-levelled books are a great way to build children's confidence and are ideal for independent reading. For more information about the levelling in **Project X *Alien Adventures***, see pages 39–41.

> For information on how to use **Project X *Alien Adventures*** to support paired reading, see page 28, (Reading partners) and for guidance on modelled reading, see page 27 (The importance of reading aloud).

Communication skills

The importance of talk and other forms of communication in developing children's literacy and wider social skills is widely recognized. The **Project X *Alien Adventures*** books have been designed to stimulate talk and there is support within the books for exploring characters, retelling stories, raising and responding to questions, and expressing opinions.

> For more information on how **Project X *Alien Adventures*** supports talking and listening, see pages 10–11, 15 and 24–29.

Using ICT

Project X *Alien Adventures* supports the creative use of ICT, emphasized in the Northern Ireland Curriculum. All of the stories feature an engaging, detailed, 3D digital illustration style. A number of **Project X *Alien Adventures*** eBooks can be accessed free online to support the development of multimedia literacy skills. The **Project X *Alien Adventures*** animations and the companion books can be used to generate excitement about the series in a class session. To watch the animations, visit: **www.oxfordprimary.co.uk**, and for more information on the companions, see pages 42–43.

Thinking, problem solving and decision making

The **Project X *Alien Adventures*** stories present readers with a range of scenarios in which our core characters are faced with problems, challenges and decisions to make. By following the adventures of Max, Cat, Ant, Tiger and Nok, readers can learn to empathize and to develop their problem-solving skills.

Assessment

Approaches to reading assessment in **Project X *Alien Adventures*** are well aligned to best practice outlined in the Northern Ireland Curriculum, particularly with regards to formative assessment. For detailed support on observation, formative assessment, and planning see pages 44–57.

Statutory Requirements for Language and Literacy in Key Stages 1 and 2

Project X *Alien Adventures* can help you deliver the following statutory requirements for *Talking and listening* and *Reading*. Inside cover notes and Photocopiable Masters (PCMs) for each book provide a range of discussion points and follow-up activities, including ideas for writing activities.

Key Stage 1

Teachers should enable pupils to develop knowledge, understanding and skills in:

Talking and listening

Pupils should be enabled to:

- participate in talking and listening in every area of learning;
- listen to, respond to and explore stories, poems, songs, drama, and media texts through the use of traditional and digital resources and recreate parts of them in a range of expressive activities;
- listen to, interpret and retell, with some supporting detail, a range of oral and written texts;
- listen to and respond to guidance and instructions;
- take turns at talking and listening in group and paired activities;
- express thoughts, feelings and opinions in response to personal experiences, imaginary situations, literature, media and curricular topics and activities;
- present ideas and information with some structure and sequence;
- think about what they say and how they say it;
- speak audibly and clearly, using appropriate quality of speech and voice;
- read aloud from a variety of sources, including their own work, inflecting appropriately to emphasize meaning.

Reading

Pupils should be enabled to:

- participate in modelled, shared, paired and guided reading activities;
- read, and be read to from a wide selection of poetry and prose;
- read with some independence for enjoyment and information;
- read, explore, understand and make use of a range of traditional and digital texts;
- retell, reread and act out a range of texts, representing ideas through drama, pictures, diagrams and ICT;
- begin to locate, select and use texts for specific purposes;
- use a range of comprehension skills, both oral and written, to interpret and discuss texts;
- explore and begin to understand how texts are structured in a range of genres;
- explore and interpret a range of visual texts;
- express opinions and give reasons based on what they have read;
- begin to use evidence from text to support their views;
- read and share their own books of stories and poems including the use of digital resources;
- build up a sight vocabulary;
- use a range of strategies to identify unfamiliar words;
- talk with the teacher about ways in which language is written down, identifying phrases, words, patterns or letters and other features of written language;
- recognize and notice how words are constructed and spelt.

Key Stage 2

Teachers should enable pupils to develop knowledge, understanding and skills in:

Talking and listening

Pupils should be enabled to:

- listen and respond to a range of fiction, poetry, drama and media texts through the use of traditional and digital resources;
- tell, retell and interpret stories based on memories, personal experiences, literature, imagination and the content of the curriculum;
- participate in group and class discussions for a variety of curricular purposes;
- know, understand and use the conventions of group discussion;
- share, respond to and evaluate ideas, arguments and points of view and use evidence or reason to justify opinions, actions or proposals;
- formulate, give and respond to guidance, directions and instructions;
- identify and ask appropriate questions to seek information, views and feelings;
- talk with people in a variety of formal and informal situations;
- use appropriate quality of speech and voice, speaking audibly and varying register, according to the purpose and audience;
- read aloud, inflecting appropriately, to express thoughts and feelings and emphasise the meaning of what they have read.

Reading

Pupils should be enabled to:

- participate in modelled, shared, paired and guided reading experiences;
- read, explore, understand and make use of a wide range of traditional and digital texts;
- engage in sustained, independent and silent reading for enjoyment and information;
- extend the range of their reading and develop their own preferences;
- represent their understanding of texts in a range of ways, including visual, oral,
  dramatic and digital;
- consider, interpret and discuss texts, exploring the ways in which language can be manipulated in order to affect the reader or engage attention;
- justify their responses logically, by inference, deduction and/or reference to evidence within the text;
- reconsider their initial response to texts in the light of insight and information which emerge subsequently from their reading;
- read aloud to the class or teacher from prepared texts, including those composed by themselves, using inflection to assist meaning;
- use a range of cross-checking strategies to read unfamiliar words in texts;
- use a variety of reading skills for different reading purposes.

Alien Adventures

Photocopiable Masters

Book Bands Brown to Grey
(Oxford Levels 9 to 14)

Whatever next?

The story *The Destroyer* ends on a cliffhanger. Max, Ant and Nok meet a rat-like creature who beckons them to follow him. Should they follow the rat? Can they trust it? Write the next episode of this exciting adventure.

Brown Book Band (Oxford Level 9) • **The Destroyer**

2 Name _____ Date _____

Comic strip

Create a comic strip of the main parts of the story. Draw pictures of the characters, and write what they are thinking or saying.

Panel 1:
- "They're going to capture us!"
- "We can't leave my parents!"
- "Squeak!"

Alien Adventures — Brown Book Band (Oxford Level 9) • **Space Rat Rescue**
© Oxford University Press 2014. Copying permitted within the purchasing school only.

3 Name _____ Date _____

Crunch that junk!

Design your own junk cruncher. It might look like a steam roller, an elephant, a shark … or something else entirely. How does it crunch the rubbish? What does it do with it then? Label all the important parts and what they do.

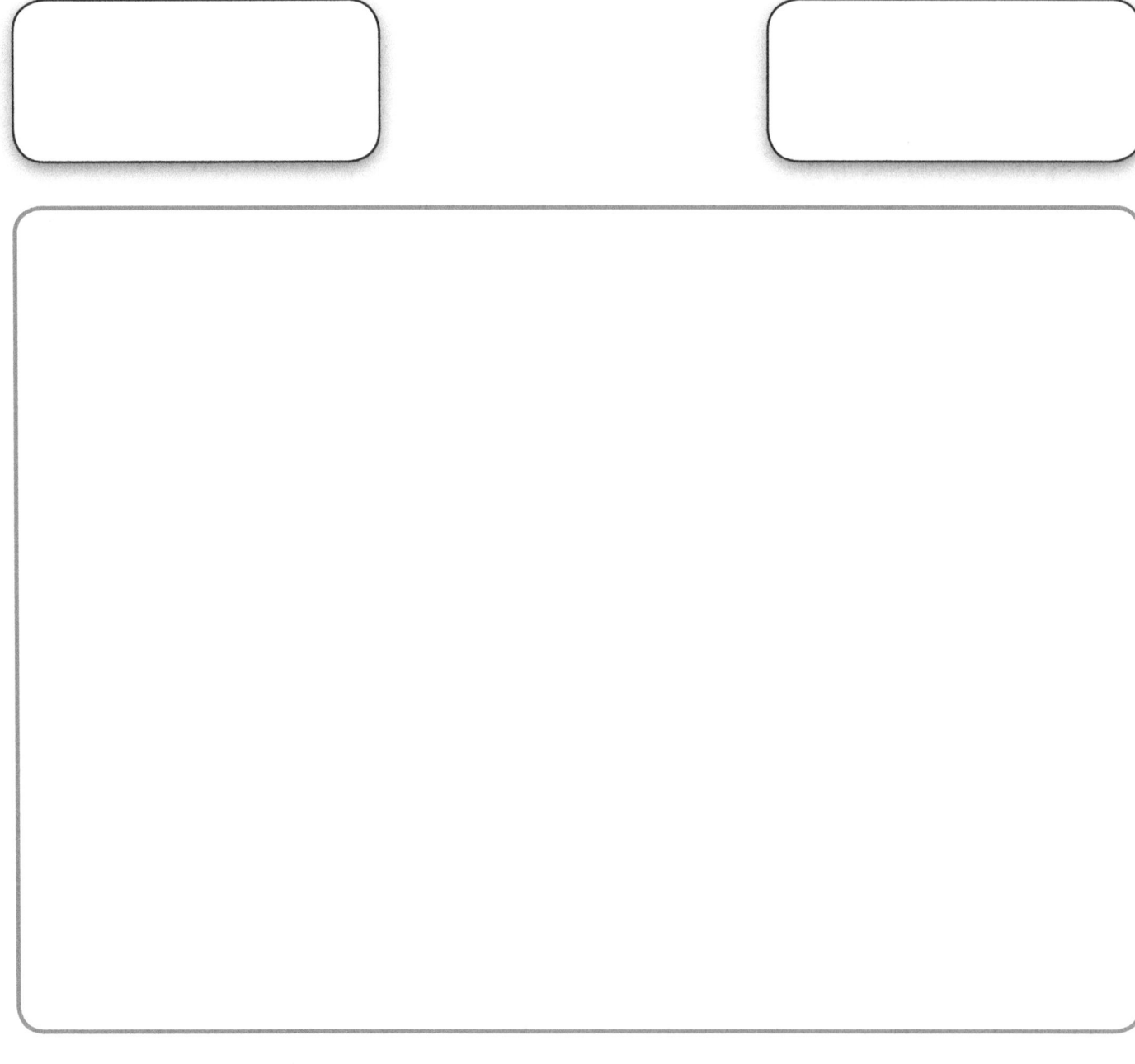

Brown Book Band (Oxford Level 9) • Crunch Time!

Problems and solutions

The friends face many problems in the story *The Moon Winder*. Explain how they solve them. The first one has been done for you.

Problem	Solution
Power levels falling	Ant runs a scan. He sees something on the outside of the ship. Ant and Tiger put on their helmets and go on a spacewalk to investigate.
Strange plant found on the outside of the ship	
Plant attacks Ant	
Moon winder will not leave until it drains all power from their ship	
The friends can't get past the plant to get off the Excelsa	
The moon winder won't let go!	

Alien Adventures — Brown Book Band (Oxford Level 9) ● **The Moon Winder**

5 Name _____ Date _____

Space vultures vs Earth vultures

Compare the vultures we have here on Earth with those in the story.

Space vultures	Earth vultures
Draw and colour a space vulture here.	Draw and colour a real vulture here.
Diet	Diet
Habitat	Habitat

Brown Book Band (Oxford Level 10) • Space Vultures

6 Name _____ Date _____

Danger!

Design an eye-catching poster to warn space travellers about the dangers of the Planet of Bones.

Tips:
- Use facts from the book.
- Describe what is scary about the planet.
- Describe what you should do if you are charged by a skelox.

Brown Book Band (Oxford Level 10) • The Planet of Bones

7 Name _____ Date _____

Word finder

Write down any new words you meet as you read the story. When you have finished the story, find out their meanings.

New word	Word meaning

Brown Book Band (Oxford Level 10) • Starmite Swarm

| 8 | Name _____ | Date _____ |

Rules for good behaviour

Ariddians are known for being mean and grumpy. Write some rules for good behaviour which will help Anko and Skiz become nicer Ariddians.

Rule no. 1
Always

Rule no. 2
Never

Rule no. 3
Don't

Rule no. 4
Try to

Rule no. 5
Try not to

Rule no. 6
Remember to

Brown Book Band (Oxford Level 10) ● **The Giants of Ariddas**
© Oxford University Press 2014. Copying permitted within the purchasing school only.

9 Name _____ Date _____

Tongue twisters

Write your own tongue-twister sentences about events or creatures in the story. Make as many words as you can begin with the same sound or letter. The first one has been done for you.

Craggrox are cranky creatures with mouths like caves.

Brown Book Band (Oxford Level 11) • The Craggrox Awake
Alien Adventures © Oxford University Press 2014. Copying permitted within the purchasing school only.

10 Name _____ Date _____

Postcard from Spongemar

Write a postcard from one of the micro-friends telling everyone at home what exciting things happened on Planet Spongemar. There is space on the front for a picture of the planet or a blob monster!

Front

Back

Place stamp here

_____

_____

_____

Brown Book Band (Oxford Level 11) • **Attack of the Blobs**
© Oxford University Press 2014. Copying permitted within the purchasing school only.

Clue quest

Sometimes an author will not tell the reader everything ... Instead clues are left to help us infer what is happening. These clues make us want to read on and find out more. Locate the sentences below in the book *The Image Maker*. Reread the sentences and the page they are on. What do you infer?

Page	Clue from the book	This makes me think that ...
p10	The door led through to a corridor. Still there was no one in sight. "Where is everybody?" said Cat uneasily.	This is very strange. Big cities are usually full of life. I can understand why Cat is uneasy. If I read on I think I will find out why!
p12	Weirdly, though, there was no noise, no music, no chatter. Not even a whisper.	
p21	"Are you all right?" asked Tiger. Nok nodded in a daze. "My parents looked so real."	
p23	Then it suddenly tossed the hose towards them like a lasso ... and caught them all together. "Hey!" Tiger shouted. "What's the big idea?" The robot only smiled.	
p35	"Sprocket will recover. But he will always be lonely. Unless ..." He looked around and smiled. "I have an idea."	

Brown Book Band (Oxford Level 11) • **The Image Maker**
© Oxford University Press 2014. Copying permitted within the purchasing school only.

12 Name _____ Date _____

Axis of emotion

Reread the story *Battle with Badlaw* and consider how you felt when you were reading the pages below. Plot your feelings on the axis of emotion below using these symbols:

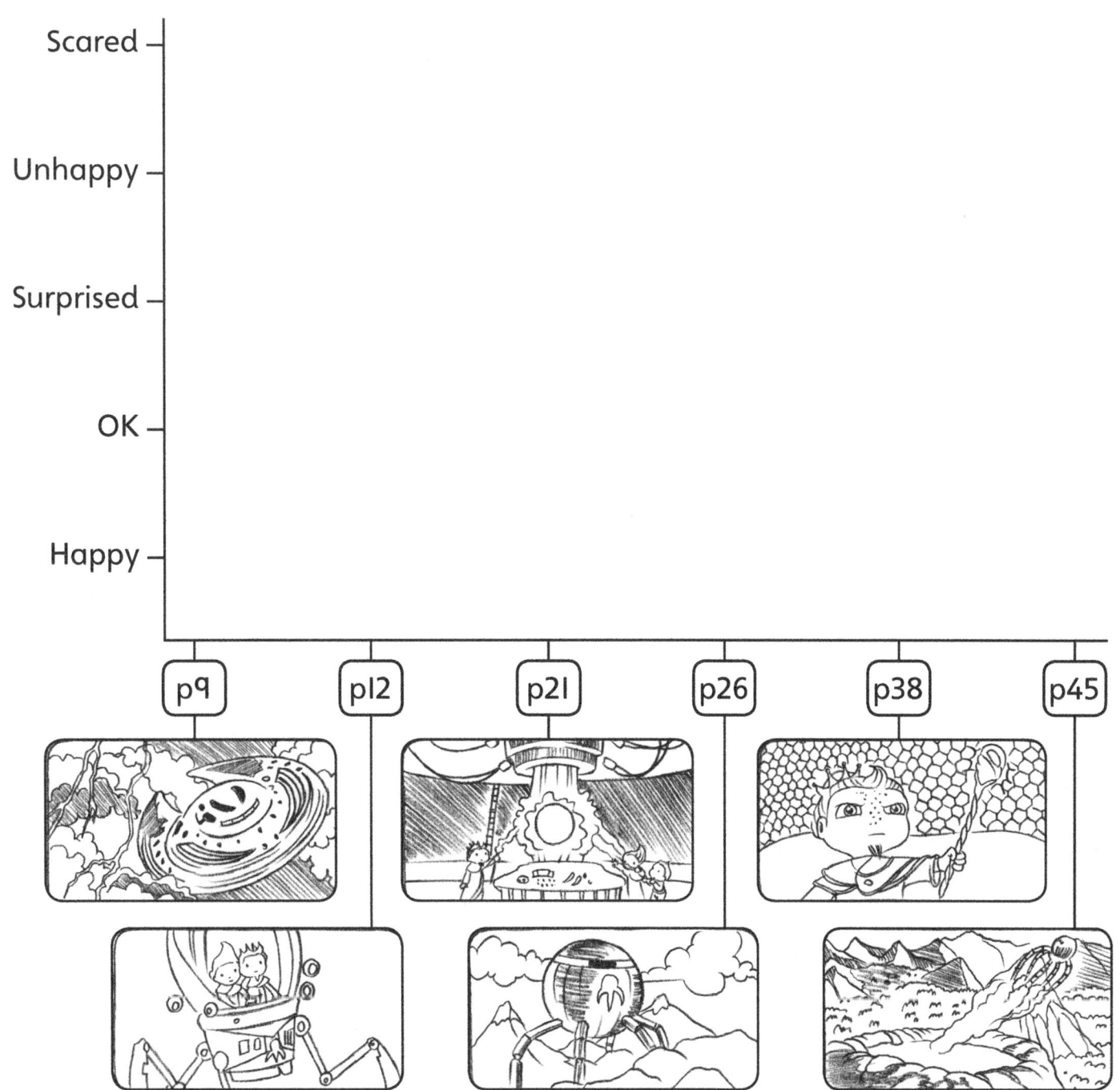

| Happy | OK | Surprised | Unhappy | Scared |

Scared –

Unhappy –

Surprised –

OK –

Happy –

p9 p12 p21 p26 p38 p45

Brown Book Band (Oxford Level 11) • **Battle with Badlaw**
© Oxford University Press 2014. Copying permitted within the purchasing school only.

Text chat

Pretend you are one of the characters on the Excelsa and you are texting a friend back on Earth. In ten words or less, outline the main things that happen in each chapter. The first one has been done for you.

At leaving party … been given a new ship and robot!

Grey Book Band (Oxford Level 12) • Badlaw's Revenge

| 14 | Name _____ Date _____ |

Create a new rat

In *The Rats of Rolia*, there are two types of rat: green rats and red rats. Imagine you have landed on a planet and met a new type of rat. How is it different from the green and red rats? Make a fact file about it.

Draw a new rat

The _____ rats of _____

_____

_____

_____

Home: _____

Work: _____

Food: _____

Character: _____

Alien Adventures Grey Book Band (Oxford Level 12) ● **The Rats of Rolia**
© Oxford University Press 2014. Copying permitted within the purchasing school only.

15 Name _____ Date _____

Questions and answers

As we read we need to ask questions about the story in our head and see if we can answer them. That way we will know if we have understood the story. Write your own questions about *Trapped in Time* as you read the story and try to find the answers. The first one has been done for you.

Q: Why are the crew on the Excelsa repeating what they are saying?

A: The time rift has something to do with it…it's like they're stuck in time and can't move on.

Q:

A:

Q:

A:

Q:

A:

Grey Book Band (Oxford Level 12) • Trapped in Time
© Oxford University Press 2014. Copying permitted within the purchasing school only.

16 Name _____ Date _____

Film frames

Imagine you are making *Double Cross* into a film. Which are the the six most important scenes you would want to include? Draw what is happening in each.

Grey Book Band (Oxford Level 12) • **Double Cross**

17

Name _____ Date _____

Escape from Rustan game

Write in the boxes the events that occur to help the friends escape from Rustan and the events that prevent them escaping. The first couple have been done for you. Play the game with a partner. You will need a dice and two counters.

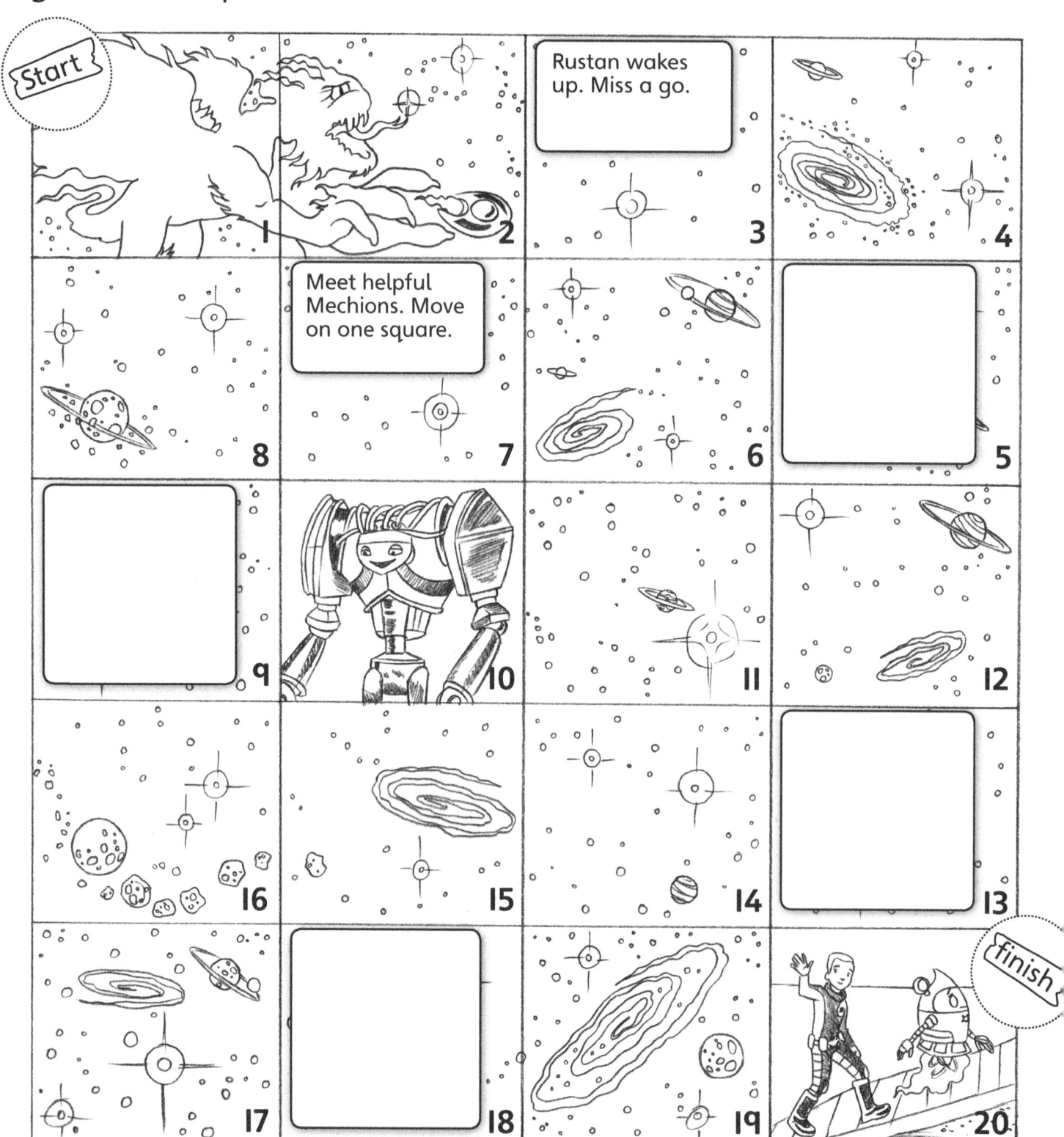

Start (1)	2	3 Rustan wakes up. Miss a go.	4
8	7 Meet helpful Mechions. Move on one square.	6	5
9	10	11	12
16	15	14	13
17	18	19	20 finish

Grey Book Band (Oxford Level 13) • The Rust Monster

Alien Adventures © Oxford University Press 2014. Copying permitted within the purchasing school only.

18 Name _____ Date _____

Let's summarize

Write some sentences which summarize the most important aspects of each chapter in *Pit-stop Peril*.

Chapter 1 – Tracked down _____

_____

Chapter 2 – Diversion _____

_____

Chapter 3 – The space garage _____

_____

Chapter 4 – A helping hand _____

_____

Chapter 5 – No more delays _____

_____

Chapter 6 – Badlaw's attack _____

_____

Chapter 7 – Escaping Badlaw _____

_____

Grey Book Band (Oxford Level 13) ● **Pit-stop Peril**
© Oxford University Press 2014. Copying permitted within the purchasing school only.

19 Name _____ Date _____

Captain Greenbeak's log

Write a page of Captain Greenbeak's ship's log. It should say what happened in *The Red Cutlass* from the captain's point of view.

Location: Delta-Zimmer Galaxy

Date: _____

Events: I couldn't have been more excited when my pirates found some treasure …

_____

_____

_____

_____

_____

Things to get the crew to do:

- polish the plank

- _____

- _____

Grey Book Band (Oxford Level 13) • **The Red Cutlass**
© Oxford University Press 2014. Copying permitted within the purchasing school only.

20

Name _____ Date _____

Planet fact file

Imagine you have landed on a new planet. Complete the fact file below. Draw and colour your planet.

Planet: _____

Information

Surface conditions

Known life forms

Grey Book Band (Oxford Level 13) • **Cyberbee Break Out**

Alien Adventures © Oxford University Press 2014. Copying permitted within the purchasing school only.

21 Name _____ Date _____

Alien fact file

Imagine you have met a new alien. Complete the fact file below. Draw and colour your alien.

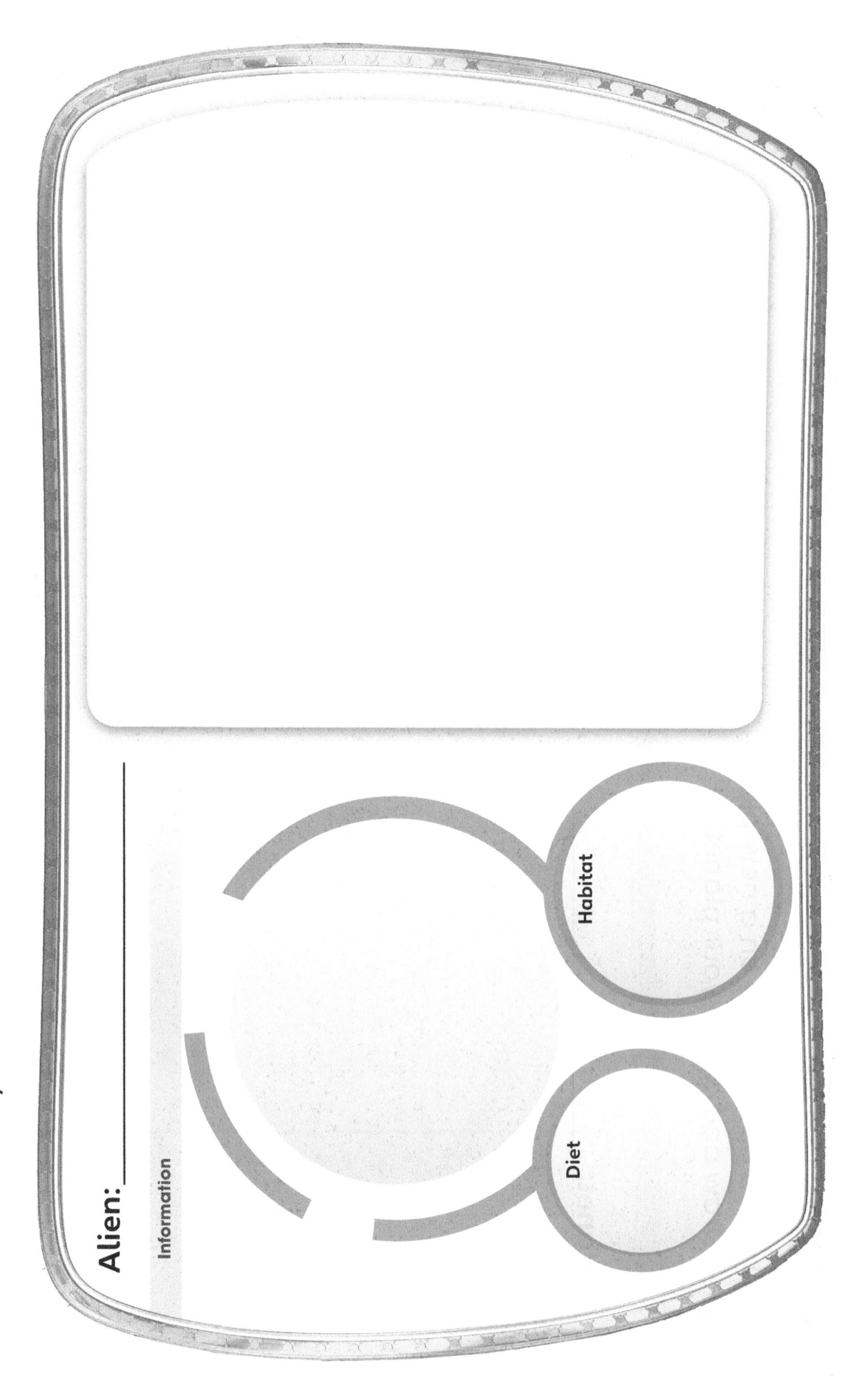

Alien: _____

Information

Habitat

Diet

Grey Book Band (Oxford Level 14) • **Operation Holotanium**

© Oxford University Press 2014. Copying permitted within the purchasing school only.

Next instalment

An Ancient Enemy ends on quite a cliffhanger. Here is how the story ends … write the next instalment.

A grinding noise echoed from behind the children.

They turned to see the bolts of the outer airlock

door sliding open … Vogoss gurgled with pleasure.

"Surrender or enjoy space oblivion!"

Grey Book Band (Oxford Level 14) ● **An Ancient Enemy**

23 Name _____ Date _____

What are they thinking?

What might the characters be thinking?
Write in the thought bubbles below.

Grey Book Band (Oxford Level 14) ● **The Fury of Vogoss**

Alien Adventures © Oxford University Press 2014. Copying permitted within the purchasing school only.

24 Name _____ Date _____

Count down

Time is ticking for the micro-friends in *The Waythroo Wormhole*. Write in the boxes below the events in the order in which they happen, from when Tiger goes in search of food, to when the Excelsa arrives on the other side of the wormhole.

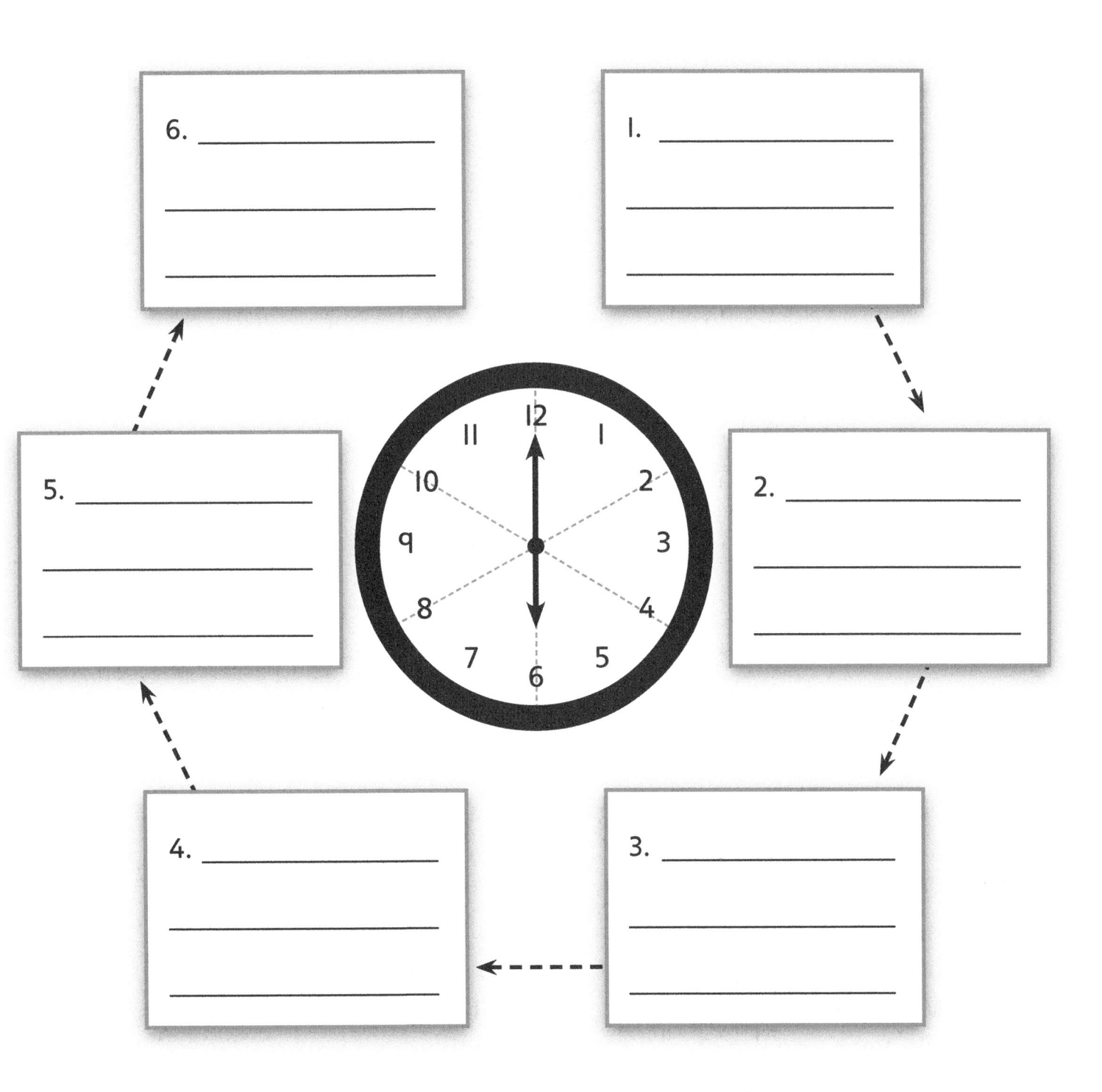

6. _____

1. _____

5. _____

2. _____

4. _____

3. _____

Grey Book Band (Oxford Level 14) ● **The Waythroo Wormhole**
© Oxford University Press 2014. Copying permitted within the purchasing school only.

Space poem

Imagine you have blasted off into space for the first time. Where are you going? What are you travelling in? Try to write a poem about your journey.

Tips:
- Close your eyes and think about the following:
  o What can you see?
  o What can you hear?
  o What can you feel?
  o What can you smell?
- Think of some words that rhyme with your answers.

26 Name _____ Date _____

Idea generator

Imagine that you have to write a story about two alien races that are battling with each other. Fill in the chart below to help you plan your story.

_____ vs _____	
Where is the story set?	
What has caused the aliens to go into battle?	
How long has the battle been going on?	
Who are the main characters?	
How is peace restored?	

27 Name _____ Date _____

What might happen?

Look at the front and back cover of a book you have not yet read. What do you think might happen? Write down your ideas in the first two columns. Read the book. Then write down what <u>did</u> happen in the last column.

Book title: _____

Author: _____

I think this might happen …	I think this because …	What did happen …

Alien Adventures © Oxford University Press 2014. Copying permitted within the purchasing school only.

28 Name _____   Date _____

New planet experience

Imagine you have been teleported on to a new planet.
Write about it and draw a picture below.

What can you see/smell/hear?
What do you feel? Why?
Who or what do you meet?
My drawing of the planet …

Alien Adventures © Oxford University Press 2014. Copying permitted within the purchasing school only.

29

Name _____ Date _____

Write a scene

Think of a story that you have read recently. Turn one of the scenes from the story into a play. You could act it out with your friends.

Character	What are they saying and/or doing?

Max   Cat   Ant   Tiger   Nok   Seven

30 Name _____ Date _____

Think, feel, say ....

During or after reading a book, make notes in the shapes below to help you form an opinion about it.

What do I think about this book?

What do I feel about this book?

What would I tell a friend about this book?

New words

Write down any new words that you encountered recently in a book. Look up their meaning, and then make up a sentence using the word.

Word	Meaning	My sentence

Exciting events

Think of a story you have read recently. What were the exciting bits? What made them exciting? List the words or phrases that helped to make them exciting.

What was the exciting event? Who was involved?	Words or phrases that helped to make it exciting ...

33 Name _____ Date _____

Storyboard

Think of a story you have read recently. Make notes or sketch the main events from each chapter.

Chapter 1 _____	Chapter 2 _____
Chapter 3 _____	Chapter 4 _____
Chapter 5 _____	Chapter 6 _____

Alien Adventures © Oxford University Press 2014. Copying permitted within the purchasing school only.

34 Name _____ Date _____

Setting, character, plot

Think of a story you have read recently. Where was it set? Who were the main characters and what were they like? What happened? Write about it in the boxes below.

Describe the setting

Describe the main character/s

Describe what happened

35 Name _____ Date _____

Wanted!

Fill in the wanted poster for a new space villain.

WANTED

Name: _____

Wanted for: _____

_____

Description: _____

_____

Cruel deeds: _____

_____

Reward: _____

36 Name _____ Date _____

Compare and contrast

Use this grid to compare and contrast information from different non-fiction sources, e.g. books, magazines, video clips, the internet.

Information source	What I found out …
1) Title	
2) Title	
3) Title	

Using information from all of your sources write a short report of what you have learned.

37 Name _____ Date _____

Heroes and villains!

Think of a character from a story who is a hero.
Then think of a villain.

Hero's name: _____

Why are they a hero?

_____

_____

_____

Villain's name: _____

Why are they a villain?

_____

_____

_____

38 Name _____ Date _____

How to make a ...

Imagine that you have to give a friend instructions on how to make a robot. How would you tell them to make it? What type of robot would it be?

Instructions to make a _____

You will need:

-
-
-
-

What you need to do:

1)

2)

3)

4)

5)

6)

7)

39 Name _____ Date _____

Character spidergram

Make a spidergram of words to describe your favourite character from a book you have read. Draw the character in the centre.

Name of character _____

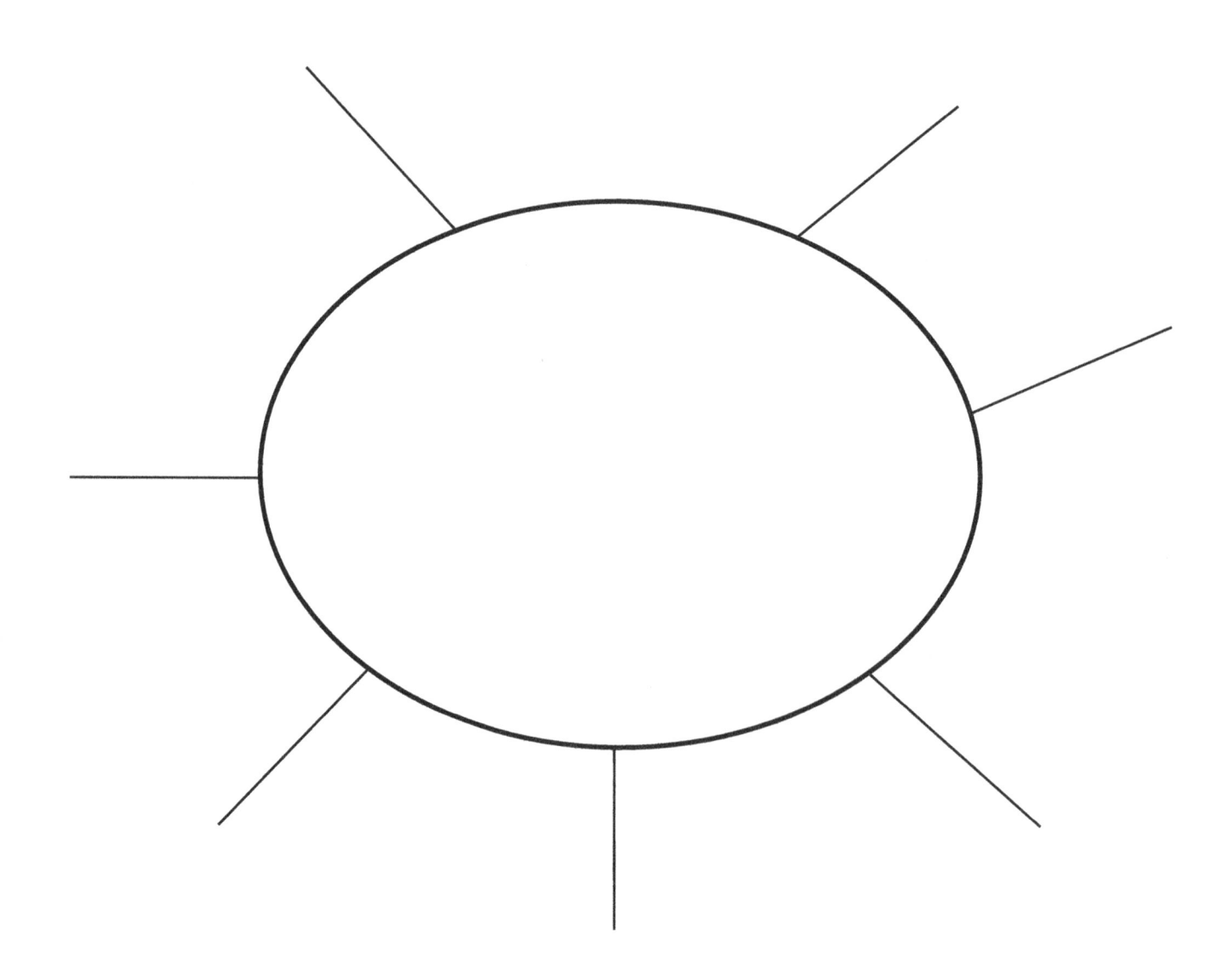

Alien Adventures © Oxford University Press 2014. Copying permitted within the purchasing school only.